Kurt Barth

Faszination Switzerland

Eine Reise durch die Schweiz
Un voyage à travers la Suisse
Un viaggio attraverso la Svizzera
A journey through Switzerland

Telldenkmal in Altdorf UR
Monument de Guillaume Tell à Altdorf UR
Monumento di Guglielmo Tell a Altdorf UR
Monument to William Tell in Altdorf UR

Umschlag vorne:
Bei Gsteig BE – Oldenhorn

Couverture devant:
Environs de Gsteig BE – Oldenhorn

Copertina in testa:
Dintorni di Gsteig BE – Oldenhorn

Front cover:
Near Gsteig BE – Oldenhorn

Vorsatz: Eiger, Mönch und Jungfrau BE

Kurt Barth

Faszination Switzerland

Eine Reise durch die Schweiz
Un voyage à travers la Suisse
Un viaggio attraverso la Svizzera
A journey through Switzerland

Text/Texte/Testo/Text: Dr. Hans Rudolf Böckli

EDITION BARTH BERN

JUSTISTAL

Inhaltsverzeichnis

Sommaire

Kästeilet im Justistal BE

Distribution du fromage dans le Justistal BE

Kästeilet nella Justistal BE (festa popolare)

Cheese sharing-out ceremony in the Justis Valley BE

Contenuto

Contents

Vorwort

Was macht die Faszination eines Landes aus? Wenn wir diese Frage auf die Schweiz übertragen, dann ist es die Vielfalt, die traditionsbewusste Lebensweise und das vielenorts mit Hingabe gepflegte Brauchtum, die Vielsprachigkeit, die reizvollen Landschaften und sehenswerten Städte, eine gepflegte Gastronomie und als Ferien- und Reiseland die in aller Welt bekannte Hotellerie. Die wirtschaftliche Bedeutung erlangte die Schweiz durch die dank privater Initiative weltweit vermarktbaren Arbeits- und Dienstleistungen von Chemie- und Maschinenindustrie, Gewerbe und Handel, Uhrenfabrikation, Banken und Versicherungen.
Wie ein Vergleich unter einundzwanzig Ländern ergeben hat, vermittelt diese Vielseitigkeit ein ausnehmend positives Image bei unseren ausländischen Gästen und Besuchern, und wir möchten diesen Eindruck mit dem Bildband noch fördern und dem Leser eine bleibende Erinnerung an unser Land mitgeben. Dem Schweizer Leser wird das Buch Erinnerungen an Ferien und Ausflüge wachrufen, und es soll ihm zugleich Anregung und Ansporn sein, wieder einmal eine der wunderschönen Regionen zu besuchen.

Der Herausgeber

Avant-propos

D'où provient la fascination exercée par un pays? En ce qui concerne la Suisse, cette fascination provient certainement de sa diversité, de son style de vie respectueux des traditions et, en de nombreux endroits, de coutumes perpétuées avec passion; mais elle provient également des différentes langues parlées dans ce pays, de ses paysages attrayants, de ses villes, de sa gastronomie soignée et de son hôtellerie renommée dans le monde entier – une hôtellerie d'un pays de vacances et de tourisme. L'importance économique de la Suisse a été acquise grâce à des initiatives privées – notamment dans l'industrie chimique et l'industrie des machines, les arts et métiers, le commerce, la fabrication de montres, les secteurs des banques et des assurances – à l'origine de produits et de services commercialisés dans le monde entier. Cette diversité laisse une image exceptionnellement favorable à nos hôtes étrangers, une impression que nous aimerions encore promouvoir par cet ouvrage, en laissant au lecteur un souvenir impérissable de notre pays. Au lecteur suisse, ce livre évoquera des souvenirs de vacances et d'excursions, qui seront autant de motivations à visiter à nouveau l'une des régions merveilleuses du pays.

L'éditeur

Prefazione

In che cosa consiste il fascino di un paese? Se rivolgessimo questa domanda alla Svizzera, ricaveremmo una miriade di risposte: il profondo legame con le tradizioni, la dedizione agli usi e costumi, il plurilinguismo, le splendide campagne e le incantevoli città, la gastronomia oltremodo curata e la notorietà delle nostre infrastrutture alberghiere e turistiche. La notorietà in materia economica, la Svizzera la deve soprattutto all'iniziativa privata. In questo ambito sono famose in tutto il mondo l'industria chimica, meccanica, orologera, le prestazioni di servizi e della manodopera, l'artigianato e il commercio, le banche e le compagnie di assicurazione. In un confronto con ventun paesi, tale versatilità incrementa l'immagine positiva che di noi hanno gli ospiti e i visitatori stranieri. Grazie a questo volume illustrato, intendiamo incentivare tali impressioni favorevoli e regalare al lettore un ricordo bello e duraturo del nostro paese. Nel lettore svizzero questo volume farà rivivere il periodo delle vacanze e delle gite. Da parte nostra speriamo che la lettura lo inciti alla riscoperta delle splendide regioni di casa nostra.

L'editore

Preface

What are the features of a country that make it fascinating? If we apply this question to Switzerland then this would be the variety, the consciousness of tradition in its way of life and the customs which are so passionately preserved in many areas of the country, the diversity of languages, the charming landscapes, the attractions of the cities, and the sophisticated cuisine and, as a holiday and travel destination, the hotel trade famous throughout the world. Switzerland achieved its commercial importance through its efficiency and the services of the chemical and machine construction industries, commerce and trade, clock and watch manufacture, banking and insurance, all marketed throughout the world thanks to the entrepreneurial spirit of the private sector.
As shown by a comparison among twenty-one countries, this variety portrays an extremely positive image amongst our foreign guests and visitors and we would like to further encourage this impression through this collection of pictures and to give the reader a permanent reminder of our country.
For the Swiss reader, the book will awaken memories of holidays and trips and act simultaneously as an encouragement and incentive to him to pay a return visit to one of the beautiful regions.

The Publisher

Reformationsdenkmal in Genf
Monument de la Réformation à Genève
Monumento della riforma a Ginevra
Monument to the Reformation in Geneva

Die Westschweiz

Die Westschweiz (GE, VD, VS, NE, FR, JU) ist grösstenteils französischsprachig. Das Rhonetal, die Abhänge zum Genfersee, das westliche Ufer des Neuenburger- und Bielersees sind berühmt für ihre Weissweine, einige Lagen im Wallis und in der Waadt auch für Rotweine. Wegen ertragreicher Früchte- und Tomatenkulturen gilt das untere Wallis als das «Kalifornien der Schweiz». Auf den Hochebenen und in den Tälern der Jurakette befinden sich Fabrikationsstandorte der Uhrenindustrie.
Genf, die drittgrösste Stadt der Schweiz, mit einem internationalen Flughafen, ist ein bedeutendes Industrie- und Bankenzentrum. Hier wurde das Rote Kreuz gegründet, und auch heute noch ist die Stadt Sitz des Internationalen Komitees vom Roten Kreuz (IKRK). Zwischen den beiden Weltkriegen beherbergte Genf den Völkerbund, in dessen monumentalen Gebäulichkeiten nachher der europäische Sitz der Vereinten Nationen untergebracht worden ist. Noch viele weitere internationale Organisationen haben in Genf ihr Hauptquartier. Das alles führt dazu, dass Genf immer wieder Tagungsort für wichtige politische Konferenzen und diplomatische Treffen ist.
In vier Städten der Westschweiz, nämlich in Genf, Lausanne, Fribourg und Neuchâchtel, befinden sich Universitäten.

Suisse occidentale

La Suisse occidentale (GE, VD, VS, NE, FR, JU) est en majeure partie francophone. La vallée du Rhône ainsi que les collines en bordure des lacs Léman, de Neuchâtel et de Bienne sont réputées pour leurs vins blancs, les vins rouges ne provenant que de quelques régions des cantons de Vaud et du Valais. Ce dernier canton, par l'abondance de ses cultures, est souvent considéré comme la «Californie de la Suisse». Les hauts plateaux et les vallées jurassiennes sont occupés par l'industrie horlogère. Genève, troisième ville du pays, avec son aéroport, est un important centre industriel et bancaire. C'est ici qu'a été fondée la Croix-Rouge, et que se trouve aujourd'hui le siège du comité international de cette institution (CICR). Entre les deux guerres, la capitale du bout du lac abrita la Société des Nations, dont l'imposant édifice devint ensuite le siège européen des Nations Unies. Plusieurs autres organisations internationales y ont aussi installé leur quartier général. D'où les nombreuses rencontres diplomatiques qui s'y déroulent.
Quatre villes de Suisse romande - Genève, Lausanne, Neuchâtel et Fribourg - possèdent des universités.

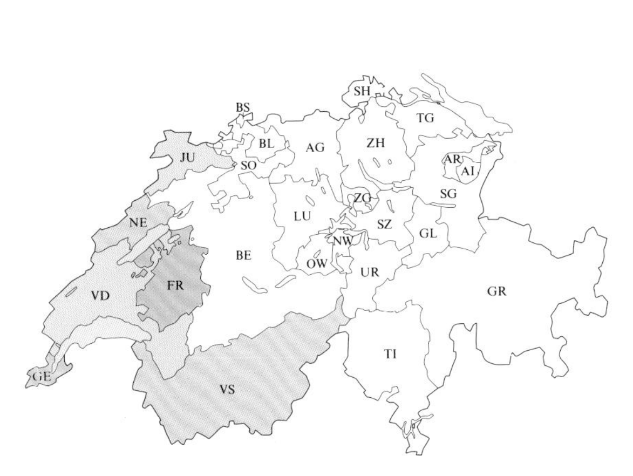

La Svizzera occidentale

La Svizzera occidentale (GE, VD, VS, NE, FR, JU) è per la maggior parte di lingua francese. La valle del Rodano, i pendii del lago di Ginevra, la riva occidentale dei laghi di Neuchâtel e di Bienne sono famosi per i loro vini bianchi, alcuni posti nel Vallese e nel Cantone di Vaud anche per i vini rossi. A causa delle abbondanti colture di frutta e di pomodori la parte inferiore del Vallese viene chiamata la «California della Svizzera». Sugli altopiani e nelle vallate della catena del Giura si trovano luoghi di fabbricazione dell'industria orologiera. Ginevra, la terza città svizzera per grandezza, con un aeroporto internazionale, è un importante centro industriale e bancario. Qui è stata fondata la Croce Rossa ed ancora oggi la città è sede del Comitato Internazionale della Croce Rossa (CICR). Nel periodo tra le due guerre, Ginevra ospitava la Società delle Nazioni; in quegli edifici monumentali è stata sistemata in seguito la sede europea delle Nazioni Unite. Molte altre organizzazioni internazionali hanno il loro quartiere generale a Ginevra. Di conseguenza, Ginevra è sempre più luogo di riunione per importanti conferenze politiche e di incontri diplomatici. In quattro città della Svizzera occidentale, cioè a Ginevra, Lausanne, Friburgo e Neuchâtel si trovano università.

Western Switzerland

Western Switzerland (the Cantons of GE, VD, VS, NE, FR, JU) is to the greatest extent French-speaking. The Rhone Valley, the slopes on the Lake of Geneva, the western shores of the lakes of Neuchâtel and Biel are famous for their white wines, some locations in the Valais and in the Vaud also for red wines.The lower part of the Valais is considered to be the 'California of Switzerland', because of its fertile lands cultivated with fruit and tomato. On the higher plateaus and in the valleys of the Jura mountain range, there are the manufacturing centres of the watchmaking industry. Geneva, the third-largest city of Switzerland, with an international airport, is an important industrial and banking centre. It is here that the Red Cross was founded and it is still today the seat of the International Committee of the Red Cross (ICRC). Between the two world wars, Geneva accommodated the League of Nations: the European headquarters of the United Nations have been housed in its monumental buildings. Many more international organizations have their headquarters in Geneva. All this has led to the fact that Geneva is time and again the venue for important political conferences and diplomatic meetings. There are universities in four cities of Western Switzerland, namely in Geneva, Lausanne, Fribourg and Neuchâtel.

Genf – Altstadt
Genève – la vieille ville
Ginevra – città antica
Geneva – old part of town

Genf mit Jet d'eau
Genève avec le jet d'eau
Ginevra con il jet d'eau
Geneva with the famous fountain

Féchy VD

Dents du Midi VS

Epesses VD

Grosser Aletschgletscher VS
Le glacier d'Aletsch VS
Il grande ghiacciaio d'Aletsch VS
The Great Aletsch Glacier VS

Ernen VS

Matterhorn VS
Le Cervin VS
Il Cervino VS
Matterhorn VS

Freiburg
Fribourg
Friburgo
Fribourg

Greyerz FR
Gruyères FR
Gruiera FR
Gruyères FR

Seite 18: Murten FR
Page 18: Morat FR
Pagina 18: Morat FR
Page 18: Morat FR

La Bosse JU

In den Freibergen JU
Dans les Franches-Montagnes JU
Nella regione delle Franches-Montagnes JU
In the Freiberge Region JU

Bern – Mittelland und Oberland

Der Kanton Bern erstreckt sich vom Zentralmassiv der Alpen quer zum Mittelland bis in die Juraketten hinein. Sein geographisches Skelett bildet die Aare mit ihren Zuflüssen und Seen. Trotz Ansätzen zur Industrialisierung – so namentlich in der Region Biel – ist der Kanton Bern ein klassisches Land der landwirtschaftlichen Produktion mit stattlichen Bauernhöfen geblieben. Der in die ganze Welt exportierte Emmentaler Käse hat hier seinen Ursprung. Die Stadt Bern ist das administrative Zentrum sowohl des Kantons wie auch der Schweiz. Seit der Errichtung des Bundesstaats (1848) ist Bern die Hauptstadt der Schweiz und Sitz ihrer Regierung, des siebenköpfigen Bundesrats. Im Bundeshaus in Bern tagen die beiden Kammern des schweizerischen Parlaments. 1191 von Berchtold V. von Zähringen gegründet, ist Bern mit seiner tadellos erhaltenen Altstadt repräsentativ für den mittelalterlichen Städtebau. Das Berner Oberland mit Thuner- und Brienzersee und seinen majestätischen Schneebergen ist ein Juwel der Alpen und als Erholungsgebiet schon früh von ausländischen Feriengästen entdeckt und bevorzugt worden. Dank unablässigem Ausbau der touristischen Infrastruktur ist es bis zum heutigen Tag ein beliebtes Fremdenverkehrszentrum geblieben.

Berne - Mittelland et Oberland

Le canton de Berne s'étend du massif central des Alpes au Plateau, jusqu'aux chaînes du Jura. Il est marqué par l'Aar, ses affluents, et ses lacs. Malgré l'industrialisation, en particulier dans la région de Bienne, le canton est demeuré un pays agricole traditionnel, aux magnifiques fermes. On y produit notamment le célèbre fromage de l'Emmenthal, exporté dans le monde entier. La ville de Berne est le centre administratif, tout à la fois du canton et de la Suisse. Depuis la constitution de la Confédération, en 1848, elle est la capitale du pays et le siège du gouvernement, fort de sept membres, et du Parlement, composé de deux chambres se réunissant plusieurs fois par an sous la coupole fédérale. Fondée par Berchtold V von Zähringen en 1191, la cité des bords de l'Aar, avec sa vieille ville soigneusement entretenue, est probablement l'une des plus belles de l'époque médié-vale. L'Oberland bernois, avec ses cimes enneigées et ses lacs de Thoune et de Brienz, est une région de villégiature réputée et appréciée, grâce au constant développement de son infrastructure touristique.

Bern – Gerechtigkeitsbrunnen
Berne – Fontaine de la Justice
Berna – Fontana della giustizia
Berne – Justice Fountain

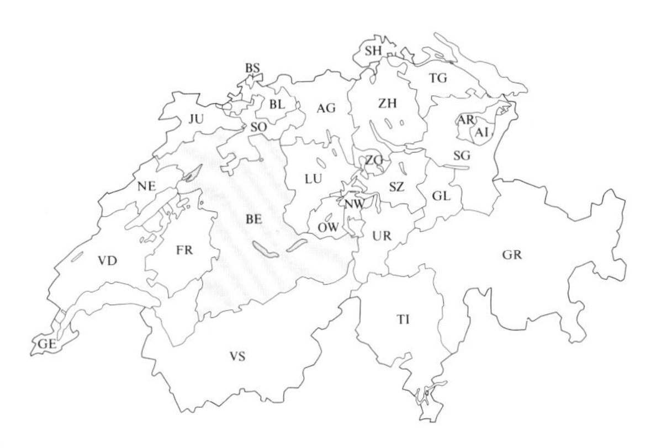

Berna - Mittelland e Oberland

Il Cantone di Berna si estende dal massiccio centrale delle Alpi, attraverso l'Altipiano, fin alla catena del Giura. Il suo scheletro geografico è formato dal fiume Aare con i suoi affluenti e dai laghi. Nonostanti alcuni inizi d'industrializzazione - soprattutto nella regione di Bienne - il Cantone di Berna è rimasto un classico paese di produzione agricola con imponenti fattorie. Il formaggio Emmental, esportato in tutto il mondo, trova qui la sua origine. La città di Berna è il centro amministrativo del Cantone così come della Svizzera. Dalla costituzione dello Stato Federale (1848), Berna è la capitale della Svizzera e la sede del governo: il Consiglio Federale composto da sette persone. Presso il Palazzo Federale a Berna si riuniscono in sessione le due Camere del Parlamento svizzero. La città di Berna, fondata nel 1191 da Berchtold V. von Zähringen, è, con la sua parte antica ben conservata, rappresentativa per l'urbanistica medioevale. Scoperto e preferito già da tempo come luogo di villeggiatura dai turisti stranieri l'Oberland bernese con il lago di Thun e di Brienz e con le sue maestose montagne coperte di neve è un gioiello delle Alpi. Grazie a un continuo sviluppo dell'infrastruttura turistica è rimasto, fino ad oggi, un centro turistico apprezzato.

Berne - Central Region and Oberland

The Canton of Berne extends from the central massif of the Alps across the Central Plain right into the mountain ranges of the Jura. Its geographical skeleton is formed by the Aare River with its tributaries and lakes. Despite rudimentary attempts at industrialization - thus particularly in the region of Biel - the Canton of Berne has remained a classical territory of agricultural production, with many stately farms. The Emmental Cheese, which is exported throughout the world, originates from these parts. The City of Berne is the administrative centre both of the Canton itself and of Switzerland. Since the establishment of the Federal State in 1848, Berne has been the capital of Switzerland and the seat of its government, the seven-member Federal Council. In the Federal Parliament Building in Berne, both chambers of the Swiss Parliament hold their sessions. Founded in the year 1191 by Berchtold von Zähringen V, Berne with its impeccably maintained old part of town is representative for medieval town building. The Bernese Oberland, with the Lakes of Thun and Brienz and its majestic snow mountains, is a gem of the Alps and was already at an early date discovered and preferred by foreign holiday visitors as a region for relaxing and recuperating.

Bern – Bundesstadt
Berne – Ville fédérale
Berna – Città federale
Berne – Federal City

Das Bundeshaus in Bern
Le Palais fédéral à Berne
Il Palazzo federale a Berna
The Federal Parliament Building in Berne

Bern – Dächer der Altstadt mit Zeitglockenturm

Berne – toits de la vieille ville avec tour de l'Horloge

Berna – tetti della città vecchia con la torre dell'Orologio

Berne – roofs of the old town and the Clock Tower

Seite 27: Bern-Land
Page 27: La campagne bernoise
Pagina 27: Berna campagna
Page 27: Rural Berne

Oben: Schloss Trachselwald
Au-dessus: château de Trachselwald
Sopra: castello Trachselwald
Top: Castle of Trachselwald

Unten: Burgdorf
Au-dessous: Berthoud
In fondo: Burgdorf
Bottom: Burgdorf

Blick auf die Berner Alpen
Vue sur les Alpes bernoises
Vista sulle Alpi bernesi
View of the Bernese Alps

Gerzensee BE

Thun mit Schloss BE
Thoune et le château BE
Tun con il castello BE
Thoune with the castle BE

Seite 30: Spiez und Schloss Oberhofen am Thunersee BE

Page 30: Spiez et le château d'Oberhofen sur le lac de Thoune BE

Pagina 30: Spiez ed il castello Oberhofen sul lago di Tun BE

Page 30: Spiez and the Castle of Oberhofen on the Lake of Thun BE

Seite 31: Blick von der First auf Wetterhorn und Schreckhorn BE
Page 31: Vue, du First, sur le Wetterhorn et le Schreckhorn BE
Pagina 31: Sguardo dal First sul Wetterhorn e Schreckhorn BE
Page 31: View from the First onto the Wetterhorn and the Schreckhorn BE

Bei Grindelwald BE
A Grindelwald BE
Presso Grindelwald BE
Near Grindelwald BE

Grimselsee BE
Le lac du Grimsel BE
Lago di Grimsel BE
Grimsel Lake BE

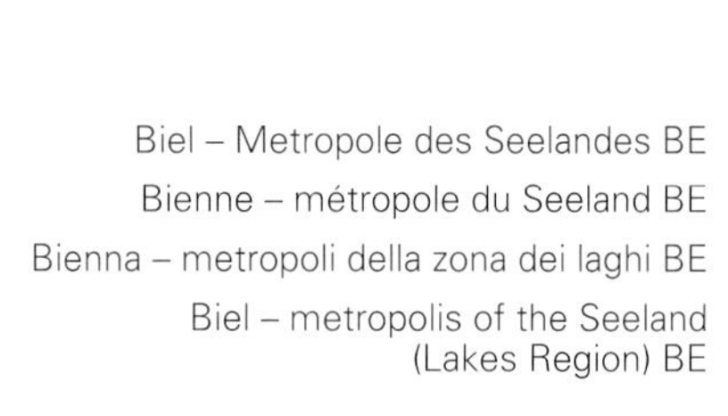

Biel – Metropole des Seelandes BE

Bienne – métropole du Seeland BE

Bienna – metropoli della zona dei laghi BE

Biel – metropolis of the Seeland (Lakes Region) BE

Erlach mit St. Petersinsel BE
Cerlier avec l'île Saint-Pierre BE
Erlach con l'isola di San Pietro BE
Erlach with the St. Peter's Peninsula BE

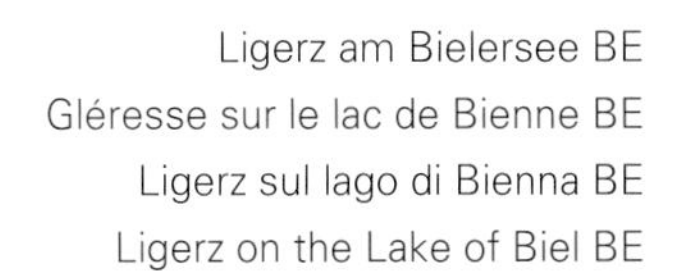

Ligerz am Bielersee BE
Gléresse sur le lac de Bienne BE
Ligerz sul lago di Bienna BE
Ligerz on the Lake of Biel BE

Lyss – zentraler Industrieort im Seeland BE,
bedeutendes Gemüseanbaugebiet

Lyss – centre industriel du Seeland BE,
région importante de culture maraîchaire

Lyss – località industriale centrale nella zona
dei laghi BE, regione importante d'orticoltura

Lyss – central industrial town
in the Seeland (Lakes Region) BE,
an important agricultural area

Die Nordwestschweiz

Nord-ouest de la Suisse

Basel – Fasnacht-Trommler
Bâle – tambours du carnaval
Basilea – carnevale-suonatore di tamburo
Basle – carnival drummers

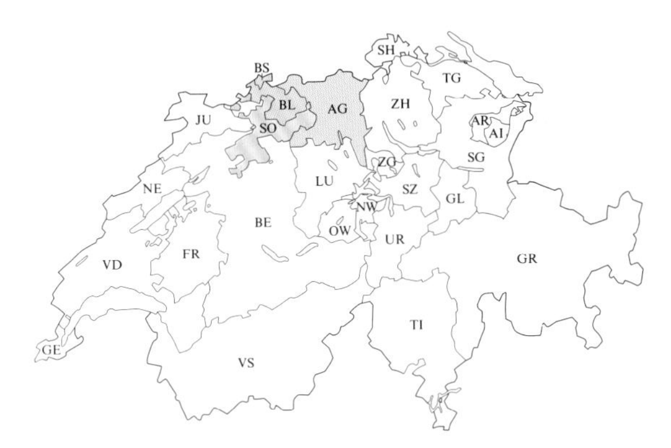

Zur Nordwestschweiz gehören vier Kantone (BS, BL, SO und AG). Das nördliche Zentrum dieses Dreiecks ist Basel, die zweitgrösste Stadt der Schweiz.
Hier war von jeher ein wichtiges Eingangstor aus Deutschland und Frankreich. Der Rheinübergang machte schon im Mittelalter aus Basel eine reiche Handelsstadt, und die 1460 gegründete erste Universität der Schweiz vermittelt bedeutsame kulturelle und wissenschaftliche Impulse. Über die Rheinschiffahrt, die in den Rheinhäfen von Basel beginnt bzw. endet, ist die Schweiz verkehrsmässig direkt mit den Meerhäfen der Nordsee verbunden. Basel ist Sitz weltbekannter Grossunternehmen der Chemie und der Bank für Internationalen Zahlungsausgleich. In den vier Kantonen dieser Region konzentrieren sich bedeutende Industrie- und Gewerbebetriebe. In diesem Gebiet sind auch vier der fünf Kernkraftwerke, die in der Schweiz in Betrieb stehen, errichtet worden, drei davon im Kanton Aargau. In den Kantonen Aargau und Solothurn sorgen bekannte Thermalquellen für regen Kurbetrieb. Oberhalb von Brugg (AG) ist das noch teilweise erhaltene Stammschloss der Dynastie der Habsburger, die Habsburg, zu besichtigen.

Ce que l'on appelle communément le nord-ouest de la Suisse est composé de quatre cantons (BS, BL, SO et AG). Le centre de la partie septentrionale de ce triangle est Bâle, deuxième plus importante ville du pays, aux portes de la France et de l'Allemagne. Sa situation privilégiée sur le Rhin en a fait une cité commerçante opulente, servant de trait d'union entre la Suisse et la mer du Nord dès le moyen âge, et son université, la première de Suisse, n'a cessé de jouer un rôle essentiel dans les domaines culturel et scientifique depuis sa fondation, en 1460. Bâle est le siège d'entreprises de la chimie mondialement connues et, notamment aussi, de la Banque des règlements internationaux. L'activité industrielle et artisanale est concentrée dans les quatre cantons de la région. C'est dans cette même région que se trouvent quatre des cinq centrales atomiques du pays, dont trois dans le seul canton d'Argovie. Ce canton et celui de Soleure sont réputés pour leurs sources thermales. En dessus de Brugg, l'on peut visiter le château d'origine, partiellement conservé, de la dynastie des Habsbourg.

NAVIS
Esso

Der Rheinhafen Kleinhüningen BS
Le port rhénan de Kleinhüningen BS
Il porto sul Reno di Kleinhüningen BS
The Rhine port of Kleinhüningen BS

La Svizzera nordoccidentale

Appartengono alla Svizzera del nordoccidentale quattro cantoni (BS, BL, SO e AG). Il centro a nord di questo triangolo è Basilea, la seconda città svizzera per ordine di grandezza. Da tempo era un'importante porta d'entrata dalla Germania e dalla Francia. Già nel Medio Evo la traversata del Reno faceva di Basilea una ricca città commerciale. La prima università della Svizzera, fondata nel 1460, le donava notevoli impulsi culturali e scientifici. Tramite la navigazione del Reno che comincia, rispettivamente finisce, nei porti sul Reno, la Svizzera, per quanto concerne la circolazione, è collegata direttamente con i porti del mare del Nord. Basilea è la sede di imprese chimiche, conosciute a livello internazionale, nonché della Banca per i regolamenti internazionali. Nei quattro cantoni di questa regione si concentrano importanti aziende industriali. In questa zona si trovano anche quattro delle cinque centrali atomiche operanti in Svizzera, tre delle quali nel Cantone Argovia. Sono possibili soggiorni di cura nelle famose sorgenti termali nei Cantoni di Argovia e di Soletta. A monte di Brugg (AG) si può visitare il castello originario, in parte ancora in buono stato, della dinastia degli Asburgo.

North-western Switzerland

Four cantons belong to north-western Switzerland (BS, BL, SO and AG). The northern centre of this triangle is Basle, the second largest city of Switzerland. Here already from time immemorial there was an important entry gate from Germany and France. The Rhine crossing already made Basle a wealthy trading city during the Middle Ages and the first university of Switzerland founded in 1460 imparts important cultural and scientific impulses. By means of the navigation on the Rhine, which starts respectively ends in the Rhine harbours of Basle, Switzerland is directly linked to seaports of the North Sea. Basle is the headquarters of world-famous major enterprises in the field of chemicals and of the Bank for International Settlements. Within the four cantons of this region, important industries and trades are concentrated. Also located in this region are four of the five nuclear power plants which are in operation in Switzerland, three of them in the Canton of Argovia. In the Cantons of Argovia and Soleure, well-known thermal springs make for a lively spa cure activity. Above Brugg (Argovia), the still partially preserved ancestrial castle of the Hapsburgs, the Habsburg, can be visited.

Fähre «Wilde Ma» auf dem Rhein BS

Le bac «Wilde Ma» sur les eaux du Rhin BS

Traghetto «Wilde Ma» sul Reno BS

Boat ferry 'Wilde Ma' (Wild Man) on the Rhine BS

Basel – Das Rathaus
Bâle – L'Hôtel de Ville
Basilea – Il Municipio
Basle – The Town Hall

Solothurn
Soleure
Soletta
Solothurn

Seite 40:
Oltingen BL – Hintergrund Wenslingen

Page 40:
Oltingen BL – à l'arrière-plan Wenslingen

Pagina 40:
Oltingen BL – sfondo Wenslingen

Page 40:
Oltingen BL – Wenslingen in the background

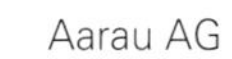

Aarau AG

Bremgarten AG

Seite 42: Olten SO

Aarburg AG

Zofingen AG – Niklaus-Thut-Platz
Zofingue AG – Place Niklaus Thut
Zofingen AG – Piazza Niklaus Thut
Zofingen AG – Niklaus Thut Square

Seite 46: Laufenburg AG

Blumenschmuck
an der Kapellbrücke in Luzern

Décoration florale
de la Kapellbrücke en Lucerne

Decorazione floreale
sul ponte della Cappella a Lucerna

Floral decorations
on the Chapel Bridge in Lucerne

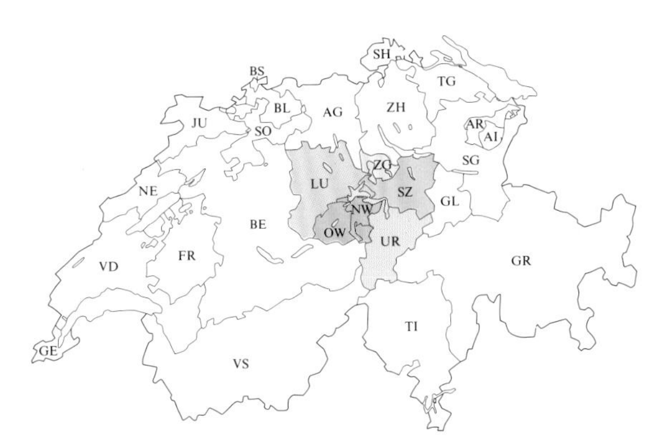

Die Zentralschweiz

Die Zentralschweiz, mit dem Vierwaldstättersee als Mittelpunkt, ist Wiege der Eidgenossenschaft, zu welcher schon früh im 14. Jahrhundert Luzern und Zug stiessen. Das wirtschaftliche Rückgrat von Uri ist der Verkehr über und durch den Gotthard, während die anderen beiden Urkantone vor allem auf der Milch- und Viehwirtschaft fussen. Die Stadt Luzern ist das natürliche Zentrum der Region und ein sehr beliebtes Reiseziel ausländischer Feriengäste. Aber auch schmucke Dörfer am nördlichen Ufer des Vierwaldstättersees und die Hotels auf dem Bürgenstock (NW) sowie der von zwei Seiten mit Bergbahnen erschlossene Rigi (SZ) laden zum Verweilen ein.
Die ganze Region bietet unzählige Zielorte für Bergfahrten und Exkursionen an. Altehrwürdige, grosse Klosteranlagen finden sich in Engelberg (OW) und in Einsiedeln (SZ), welche letztere mit einer schwarzen Madonna in der Klosterkirche ein Wallfahrtsort ist. Alle fünf Jahre wird auf dem Vorplatz dort von Laienspielern «Das grosse Welttheater» von Calderon aufgeführt. In Altdorf (UR) finden im Sommer Aufführungen des Dramas «Wilhelm Tell» statt. Im Bundesarchiv zu Schwyz sind die Freiheits- und Bundesbriefe der alten Schweizer im Original ausgestellt.

Suisse centrale

La Suisse centrale, autour du lac des Quatre-Cantons, est le berceau de la Confédération, à laquelle se sont joints, dès le 14e siècle, Lucerne et Zoug. Alors que l'activité économique d'Uri repose essentiellement sur le trafic du col du Gothard, celle des deux autres cantons primitifs est axée sur la production de lait et de bétail.
La ville de Lucerne, centre naturel de la région, est un haut lieu touristique. Mais les ravissants petits villages de la rive septentrionale du lac ainsi que, par exemple, les hôtels du Bürgenstock (NW) et le Rigi (SZ), desservis par des remontées mécaniques, invitent aussi à la découverte. On admirera en particulier deux imposants couvents, l'un à Engelberg (OW) et l'autre à Einsiedeln (SZ), réputé pour sa madone noire, et où, tous les cinq ans, sur le parvis de l'édifice, un groupe théâtral amateur joue la fameuse pièce «Le Grand Théâtre du monde», de Calderon. Et chaque été, à Altdorf (UR), on peut assister à la représentation du drame de «Guillaume Tell».
Les documents originaux de l'ancienne Suisse, tels que les lettres de franchise et le célèbre pacte, sont exposés aux Archives fédérales de Schwyz.

La Svizzera centrale

La Svizzera centrale, con il lago di Lucerna come punto centrale, è la culla della Confederazione, con cui confinavano già nel 14° secolo Lucerna e Zugo. La spina dorsale di Uri è il traffico oltre e attraverso il Gottardo, mentre gli altri cantoni primitivi si basano soprattutto sull'industria casearia e sull'allevamento di bestiame. La città di Lucerna è il centro naturale della regione e una meta di viaggio molto gradita dai turisti. Però, anche alcuni graziosi paesi sulla riva nord del lago di Lucerna e l'albergo sul Bürgenstock (NW) nonché il Rigi (SZ), racchiuso su due lati dalla ferrovia di montagna, invitano a trattenersi. L'intera regione offre numerose mete per viaggi in ferrovia e per escursioni. Considerabili per le antichità, grandi conventi si trovano a Engelberg (OW) e a Einsiedeln (SZ), quest'ultimo avendo una madonna nera nella chiesa del convento è diventato un luogo di pellegrinaggio. Sulla piazza antistante tutti i cinque anni viene rappresentato da attori laici «Il grande Teatro Mondiale» di Calderon. In estate hanno luogo a Altdorf (UR) rappresentazioni del dramma «Guglielmo Tell». Nell'archivio federale di Svitto sono esposti l'originale delle lettere di libertà e quelli federali degli antichi svizzeri.

Central Switzerland

Central Switzerland, with the Lake of Lucerne at its centre, is the cradle of the Swiss Confederation, which in the 14th century was joined by Lucerne and Zug. The economical backbone of the Canton of Uri is the traffic over and through the Gotthard, while the other two founding cantons base their economy on dairy farming and cattle breeding. The City of Lucerne is the natural centre of the region and also a very popular holiday destination for foreign visitors. But also pretty villages on the north shores of the Lake of Lucerne and the hotels on the Bürgenstock (NW), as well as the Rigi Mountain (SZ), which is made accessible by mountain railways from two sides, invite you to linger a while. The whole region offers innumerable destinations for mountain trips and excursions. Venerable old, large monasteries can be found in Engelberg (OW) and in Einsiedeln (SZ), the latter a place of pilgrimage with its Black Madonna in the monastery church. Every five years on its forecourt 'The Grand Theatre of the World' by Calderon is performed there by lay actors. In Altdorf (UR), during the summertime performances of the drama 'William Tell' take place. In the Federal Archives in the town of Schwyz, the original old Charters of Freedom and the Federal Charter of the old Swiss confederates are on exhibition.

Luzern – Kapellbrücke mit Wasserturm

Lucerne – pont de la Chapelle avec tour d’Eau

Lucerna – ponte della Cappella
con la torre d’Acqua

Lucerne – Chapel Bridge and the Water Tower

Weggis LU

Bürgenstock NW in der Abendsonne
Le Bürgenstock au coucher du soleil NW
Bürgenstock NW al tramonto
Bürgenstock NW in the evening light

Seite 51: Blick von Rigi-Kulm SZ auf den Pilatus OW
Page 51: Vue sur le Rigi SZ et le Pilate OW
Pagina 51: Sguardo dal Rigi-Kulm al Pilatus OW
Page 51: View from Rigi-Kulm (Rigi-Summit) towards the Pilatus OW

Morgenstimmung auf dem Rigi SZ
Atmosphère matinale sur le Rigi SZ
Atmosfera di mattina sul Rigi SZ
Early morning atmosphere on the Rigi SZ

Willerzell SZ

Einsiedeln SZ

Die Nordostschweiz

Die Nordostschweiz unterteilt sich in die Metropole Zürich, die weitaus grösste Stadt der Schweiz, in die Industriezentren von Winterthur und Schaffhausen sowie in die ländlichen Gebiete der Kantone Zürich und Thurgau zwischen Limmat, Rhein und Bodensee. In den letzteren befinden sich neben ausgedehnten Steinobstkulturen auch da und dort Rebberge, die einen von Kennern geschätzten Landwein hervorbringen. Der Kanton Zürich zeichnet sich unter anderem durch eine stark exportorientierte Maschinenindustrie aus, während die Stadt Zürich – mit dem grössten internationalen Flughafen der Schweiz – als bedeutender Handels- und Börsenplatz und durch seine Banken und vielfältigen Dienstleistungsbetriebe mit der Welt eng verbunden ist. Zürich ist der bevölkerungsreichste Kanton mit zwei Hochschulen und hat in wirtschaftlicher und politischer Beziehung grosse Bedeutung. Der Kanton Schaffhausen, seit 1501 der Schweiz zugehörig, ist – von Basel-Stadt abgesehen – das einzige Schweizer Territorium auf der rechten Seite des Rheins, der ansonsten die Grenze zu Deutschland markiert. Die grösste Attraktion dieses Kantons ist der imposante Rheinfall bei Neuhausen, dessen tosende Wassermassen von beiden Ufern besichtigt werden können.

Nord-est de la Suisse

Le nord-est de la Suisse englobe la métropole zurichoise, de loin la plus grande ville du pays, les centres industriels de Winterthur et de Schaffhouse, ainsi que les régions rurales des cantons de Zurich et de Thurgovie, entre la Limmat, le Rhin et le lac de Constance. Dans ces régions aux abondantes productions de fruits à noyau, on cultive également, ici et là, des vignobles donnant un vin de terroir apprécié. Alors que le canton de Zurich dispose notamment d'une industrie des machines essentiellement orientée vers l'exportation, la ville de Zurich, qui possède le plus grand aéroport international de Suisse, est une importante place commerciale et boursière, ouverte sur le monde par ses banques et ses entreprises de services. Zurich, avec ses deux hautes écoles, est le canton le plus peuplé et, politiquement, l'un des plus importants. Quant au canton de Schaffhouse, rattaché à la Confédération en 1501, il est le seul, sur la rive droite du Rhin - à part Bâle-Ville - dont la frontière jouxte, sur toute sa longueur, celle de l'Allemagne. Les chutes bouillonnantes de ce grand fleuve, vues des deux rives, près de Neuhausen, sont certainement l'attraction la plus spectaculaire du canton.

Zürich – Rathauswache
Zurich – Sentinelle de l'Hôtel de Ville
Zurigo – Sentinella di Municipio
Zürich – Town Hall Guardhouse

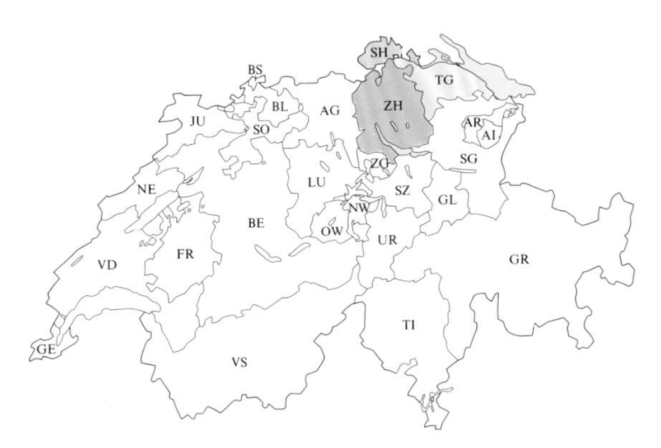

La Svizzera del nord-est

La Svizzera del nord-est comprende la metropoli di Zurigo, di gran lunga la città più grande della Svizzera, i centri industriali di Winterthur e di Sciaffusa, nonché le regioni rurali del Cantone di Zurigo e di Turgovia tra la Limmat, il Reno ed il lago di Costanza. Presso questi ultimi si trovano, oltre a estesi frutteti, qua e là anche vigneti, i quali danno un vino locale apprezzato dai conoscitori.
Il Cantone di Zurigo si distingue, tra l'altro, per l'industria meccanica fortemente orientata verso l'esportazione, mentre la città di Zurigo - con il più grande aeroporto internazionale della Svizzera - quale importante piazza borsistica e commerciale e tramite le sue banche e numerose aziende del settore terziario, è collegata strettamente con il mondo. Zurigo è il cantone con la maggior densità di popolazione, due università e ha grande importanza nei rapporti economici e politici. Il Cantone di Sciaffusa, che fa parte, dal 1501, della Svizzera, è - visto da Basilea città - l'unico territorio svizzero sulla parte destra del Reno, che marca altrimenti il confine con la Germania. La più grande attrazione di questo Cantone è l'imponente cascata presso Neuhausen, le cui fragorose masse d'acqua possono essere ammirate da entrambe le rive.

North-eastern Switzerland

North-eastern Switzerland is split-up into the metropolis of Zürich, by the largest city of Switzerland, far the industrial centres of Winterthur and Schaffhausen, as well as the rural regions of the Cantons of Zürich and Thurgovia between the Limmat and Rhine rivers and Lake Constance. In the latter regions – apart from extended stone fruit cultivation – there are here and there also vineyards, which produce a country-style wine, very highly esteemed by connoisseurs. The Canton of Zürich is distinguished by a strongly export-oriented mechanical industry, while the City of Zürich – with the biggest international airport of Switzerland – is closely linked to the world as an important commercial and stock-exchange centre, as well as by its banks and manifold service enterprises. Zürich is the canton with the largest population, with two universities, and it has a great significance in economical and political respects. The Canton of Schaffhausen, belonging to Switzerland since 1501, is – apart from Basle-City – the only Swiss territory located on the righthand side of the Rhine, which otherwise marks the border with Germany. The greatest attraction of this canton are the imposing Rhine Falls at Neuhausen, the thundering masses of water of which can be viewed from both shores of the Rhine.

Flughafen Zürich-Kloten
Aéroport de Zurich-Kloten
Aeroporto Zurigo-Kloten
Airport of Zürich-Kloten

Seite 58:
Zürich – Impressionen aus der grössten Stadt der Schweiz mit Grossmünster…

Page 58:
Zurich – impressions de la plus grande ville de Suisse, avec le Grossmünster…

Pagina 58:
Zurigo – impressioni della più grande città della Svizzera con il Grossmünster…

Page 58:
Zürich – impressions of the biggest city of Switzerland with the Grossmünster Cathedral…

swissair
A44

OMEGA

... Fraumünster und St. Peter

... le Fraumünster et l'église Saint-Pierre

... Fraumünster e San Pietro

... Fraumünster and Saint Peter's Church

Regensberg ZH

Boppelsen ZH

Schaffhausen mit Munot
Schaffhouse avec le Munot
Sciaffusa con il Munot
Schaffhausen with the Munot Tower

Stein am Rhein SH

Haus in Appenzell
Maison en Appenzell
Casa in Appenzello
House in Appenzell

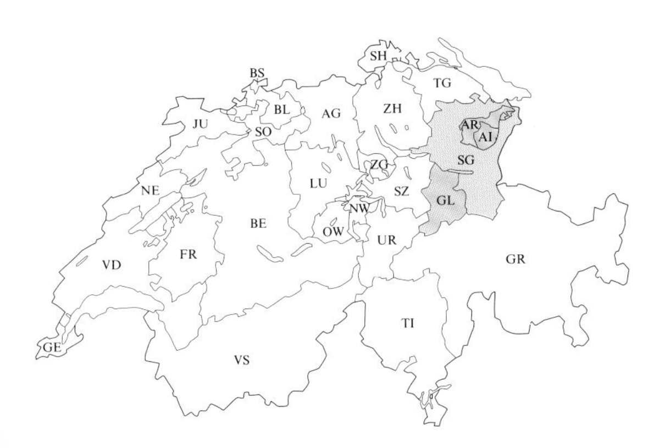

Die Ostschweiz

Den östlichen Teil der Schweiz bestreiten die Kantone St. Gallen, Appenzell und Glarus. St. Gallen wurde nach dem irischen Mönch Gallus benannt. Von hier aus ist die Schweiz im wesentlichen für das Christentum gewonnen worden. Während des ganzen Mittelalters war das Kloster St. Gallen ein geistliches Zentrum mit grosser Ausstrahlung. Noch heute zeugt die Stiftsbibliothek in St. Gallen von der Gelehrsamkeit und Kunstbeflissenheit, welcher man sich hier widmete. Die Stadt St. Gallen entwickelte sich zu einem bedeutenden Zentrum des Handels und der Industrie, namentlich im Textilbereich. Der Kanton zeichnet sich, von einigen Industriezentren abgesehen, durch eine blühende Landwirtschaft aus. Das wird heute durch eine jedes Jahr in St. Gallen abgehaltene Landwirtschaftsmesse (Olma) dokumentiert. Der Kanton Appenzell führt trotz seiner Kleinheit ein bemerkenswertes Eigenleben. Hier – wie in Glarus – versammeln sich sämtliche Stimmbürger alljährlich zu einer «Landsgemeinde», an welcher alle anstehenden Volksabstimmungen und Wahlen mit Handmehr direkt entschieden werden. Der Kanton Glarus, frühzeitig industrialisiert und sozial aufgeschlossen, ist nach Zürich hin orientiert.

Suisse orientale

La partie orientale de la Suisse comprend les cantons de Saint-Gall, Appenzell et Glaris. Saint-Gall doit son nom au moine irlandais Gallus. C'est en particulier d'ici que la Suisse a été convertie au christianisme. Le couvent de Saint-Gall fut, durant tout le moyen âge, un centre spirituel d'un grand rayonnement. Aujourd'hui encore, la bibliothèque de la collégiale atteste de l'attention que l'on portait alors à l'érudition et à la création artistique. La ville de Saint-Gall est devenue, au fil de son histoire, un important centre industriel et commercial, notamment dans le secteur textile.
Le canton, hormis ses quelques centres industriels, se distingue par son agriculture florissante. C'est ainsi que l'on peut y visiter, dans le chef-lieu, chaque année, la fameuse foire agricole de l'Olma.
Le canton d'Appenzell, malgré l'exiguïté de son territoire, a su conserver ses us et coutumes. Les citoyens, à l'instar de ceux de Glaris, se réunissent ici chaque année en «Landsgemeinde». Toutes les votations et toutes les élections se font à main levée.
Le canton de Glaris, industrialisé de longue date et socialement très avancé, est orienté vers Zurich.

La Svizzera dell'est

I Cantoni di San Gallo, d'Appenzello e di Glarona si contendono la parte est della Svizzera. San Gallo prende il nome dal monaco irlandese. Da qui la Svizzera è stata essenzialmente conquistata dal Cristianesimo. Durante l'intero Medio Evo il convento di San Gallo era un centro religioso di grande influenza. Ancora oggi la biblioteca dell'Abbazia di San Gallo rivela l'erudizione e lo studio dell'arte a cui ci si dedica. La città di San Gallo si sviluppava in un centro importante del commercio e dell'industria, esattamente del campo tessile. Il Cantone si distingue, a parte alcuni centri industriali, per la sua fiorente agricoltura. Testimonianza di ciò è attualmente l'annuale fiera dell'agricoltura (Olma) che si tiene a San Gallo. Il Cantone Appenzello, nonostante il suo piccolo territorio, ha una propria vita degna di nota. Qui - come a Glarona - si riuniscono annualmente tutti i cittadini con diritto di voto per una «Landsgemeinde», alla quale, per alzata di mano, vengono votate direttamente tutte le iniziative ed elezioni. Il Cantone di Glarona, industrializzato da tempo e socialmente ricettivo, è orientato verso Zurigo.

Eastern Switzerland

The eastern part of Switzerland is made up of the Cantons of St. Gall, Appenzell and Glarus. St. Gall was named after the Irish monk Gallus. Starting out from here, Switzerland was in essence won over to Christianity. During the whole of the Middle Ages, the Monastery of St. Gall was a spriritual centre with an extensive charisma. Even today, the collegiate library in St. Gall bears testimony to the learning and devotion to the arts to which people dedicated themselves here. The City of St. Gall developed into an important centre of trade and industry, particularly in the field of textiles. The canton is, apart from a few industrial centres, distinguished by a flourishing agriculture. This is documented by an agricultural fair (Olma), which is held every year in St. Gall. The Canton of Appenzell has a quite remarkable life of its own despite its small size. Here – as is the case in Glarus – all voting citizens meet every year for a 'Landsgemeinde' (assembly of all voters), at which all pending popular ballots and elections are decided by a direct show of hands. The Canton of Glarus, industrialized already at an early stage and socially open-minded, is oriented towards Zürich.

Sennen beim «Schellenschütteln»

Traditions alpestres

Pastori che «scampanellano»

Alpine farmers performing a cowbell-ringing ceremony

Schwellbrunn AR –
das höchstgelegene Appenzellerdorf

Schwellbrunn AR –
le village appenzellois le plus élevé en altitude

Schwellbrunn AR –
il paese di Appenzello il più in alto

Schwellbrunn AR –
the highest village of Appenzell

Appenzeller beim Alpaufzug
Appenzellois lors de la montée à l'alpage
Appenzello con corteo alpino
Appenzell people on the trail up to the Alpine pastures

Haus in Hemberg SG
Maison à Hemberg SG
Casa in Hemberg SG
House in Hemberg SG

Blick vom Käserrugg auf den Walensee SG
Vue de Käserrugg sur le Walensee SG
Sguardo dal Käserrugg sul Walensee SG
View from the Käserrugg onto the Walensee SG

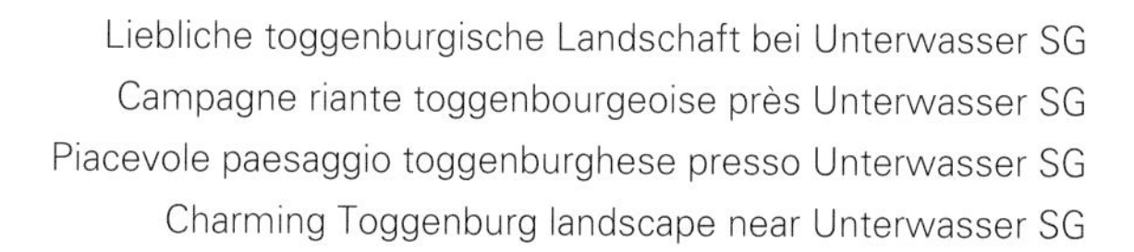

Liebliche toggenburgische Landschaft bei Unterwasser SG
Campagne riante toggenbourgeoise près Unterwasser SG
Piacevole paesaggio toggenburghese presso Unterwasser SG
Charming Toggenburg landscape near Unterwasser SG

Stiftskirche in St. Gallen
Collégiale à Saint-Gall
Collegiata a San Gallo
Collegiate Church of St. Gall

Stiftsbibliothek
Bibliothèque de la collégiale
Biblioteca del convento
Collegiate Library

Rapperswil SG

Graubünden und Tessin

Grisons et Tessin

Erker in Sent GR
Encorbellement d'une maison, à Sent GR
Sporto a Sent GR
Oriel in Sent GR

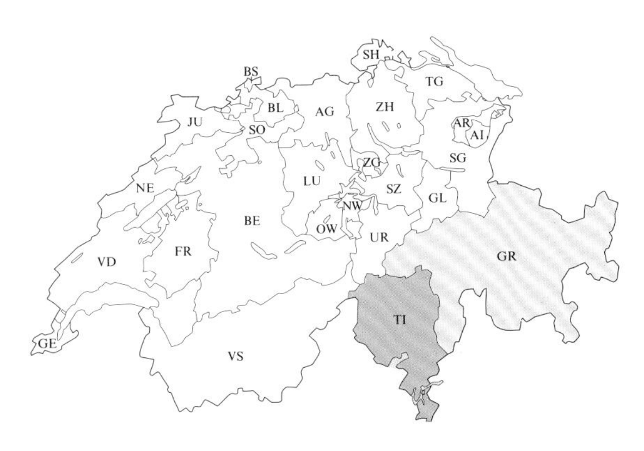

Graubünden ist flächenmässig der grösste Kanton, in welchem drei offizielle Sprachen gesprochen werden. Hier, mitten in den Alpen, liegen auch die Quellen des Rheins. Es gibt hier eine dreifache Wasserscheide: Der Rhein zieht zur Nordsee, der Inn in die Donau und damit ins Schwarze Meer und die Gewässer der südlichen Täler fliessen in den Po und damit in die Adria. Einige der landschaftlich eindrucksvollsten Gegenden der Schweiz finden sich in diesem Kanton. Aber mit Ausnahme der klimatisch begünstigten Region unterhalb von Chur, wo eine ausgezeichnete Sorte Rotwein wächst, eignet sich Graubünden fast nur für extensive Landwirtschaft und für Forstwirtschaft. Um so wichtiger sind die Einnahmen aus Wasserkraft und Fremdenverkehr. St. Moritz, Davos und Arosa zum Beispiel sind zu weitherum bekannten Zentren des Wintersports und der Sommerfrische geworden, wo sich Gäste aus aller Welt begegnen. Den Süden der Schweiz bildet der italienischsprachige Kanton Tessin, der seinerseits eine der beliebtesten Feriengegenden Europas ist. Die Nähe von Mailand und Oberitalien verschafft dem Tessin aber auch in wirtschaftlicher Beziehung einen belebenden Bonus.

On parle trois langues officielles dans les Grisons, le plus grand canton de Suisse par sa superficie. C'est ici, au cœur des Alpes, que le Rhin prend sa source. Et c'est ici également que se dessine une triple ligne de partage des eaux: celle du Rhin, qui monte vers la mer du Nord, celle de l'Inn, qui se jette dans le Danube, puis dans la mer Noire, et enfin celle des vallées du sud, qui descend dans le Pô, puis dans l'Adriatique.
Et enfin, c'est ici également que l'on peut admirer quelques-uns des paysages les plus spectaculaires de Suisse. Hormis la région viticole, en contrebas de Coire, réputée pour son vin rouge, les Grisons tirent leurs principales ressources de la culture extensive et des forêts. Les recettes de l'exploitation de l'énergie hydraulique et du tourisme n'en sont dès lors que plus appréciables. Saint-Moritz, Davos et Arosa, notamment, sont des stations de sport et de villégiature célèbres dans le monde entier. Plus au sud, le canton du Tessin, italophone, est l'une des régions d'Europe les plus prisées des vacanciers. Son essor économique est dû en particulier à la proximité de Milan et du nord de l'Italie.

Grigioni e Ticino

I Grigioni sono, per estensione di superficie, il più grande Cantone, nel quale vengono parlate tre lingue ufficiali. Qui, in mezzo alle Alpi, si trovano le sorgenti del Reno. C'è un triplo spartiacque: il Reno scorre verso il Mare del Nord, l'Inn sfocia nel Danubio, e quindi nel Mar Nero, e le acque delle vallate a sud sfociano nel Po e quindi nell'Adria. In questo Cantone si trovano alcune delle regioni dai paesaggi di più grande effetto. Però, eccezion fatta per la regione con clima favorevole sotto Coira, dove cresce un'uva per un ottimo vino rosso, i Grigioni si adattano quasi esclusivamente per l'estensiva agricoltura e per l'economia forestale. Altrettanto importanti sono gli introiti dall'energia idrica e dal turismo. St. Moritz, Davos, Arosa, per esempio, dove s'incontrano ospiti da tutte le parti del mondo, sono di gran lunga diventati famosi centri per lo sport invernale, nonché per godere la frescura estiva. Il Cantone Ticino di lingua italiana rappresenta il Sud della Svizzera ed è una delle regioni per vacanze più apprezzate d'Europa. La vicinanza con Milano e con l'Italia del Nord arreca al Ticino, però, anche uno stimolante punto in più per quanto riguarda l'economia.

Grisons and Ticino

The Canton of Grisons is the largest canton by surface area and in it three official languages of Switzerland are spoken. Here, in the midst of the Alps, the sources of the Rhine are also to be found. There is also a threefold water divide: The Rhine flows to the North Sea, the Inn into the Danube and therefore into the Black Sea, and the waters of the southern valleys join the River Po and therefore flow into the Adriatic Sea. Some of the most impressive scenery in Switzerland is to be found in this canton. But with the exception of the climatically favoured region below Chur, where incidentally an excellent type of red wine is grown, the Grisons is only suitable for extensive agriculture and forestry. This makes the income derived from hydro-electric power and from tourism all the more important. St. Moritz, Davos and Arosa, for example, have developed into widely renowned centres for winter sports and summer holiday resorts too, where visitors from all over the world meet. The southern part of Switzerland is ormed by the Italian-speaking Canton of Ticino, which for its part is one of the most popular holiday regions of Europe. The proximity to Milan and Northern Italy, however, also provides Ticino with an enlivening bonus in an economical respect.

Blick von Muottas Muragl auf St. Moritz
und die oberengadiner Seenlandschaft GR

Vue, de Muottas Muragl, sur Saint-Moritz
et sur un paysage de lacs de la haute Engadine GR

Sguardo da Muottas Muragl su San Moritz
e sul paesaggio di laghi dell'alta Engadina GR

View from Muottas Muragl onto St. Moritz
and the Upper Engadine landscape of lakes GR

Häuser in Schuls GR
Maisons à Schuls GR
Case a Schuls GR
Houses in Schuls GR

Bernina mit Morteratschgletscher GR
Col de la Bernina avec le glacier de Morterat GR
Bernina con il ghiacciaio Morteratsch GR
Bernina with the Morteratsch Glacier GR

Die romantische Schlucht Via Mala GR
La pittoresque gorge de Via Mala GR
La gola romantica Via Mala GR
The wildly romantic Via Mala Gorge GR

Igels im Lugnez GR
Igels, dans la vallée de Lugnez GR
Igels a Lugnez GR
Igels in the Lugnez Valley GR

Vogorno TI

Seite 80: Vereinatal (Alp Novai)
mit Silvrettagruppe GR

Page 80: Vereinatal (Alp Novai)
et le massif de Silvretta GR

Pagina 80: Vereinatal (Alp Novai)
con gruppo Silvretta GR

Page 80: Vereina Valley (Novai alpine pasture)
with the Silvretta Mountain Group GR

Doppelbogenbrücke bei Lavertezzo TI
Pont à double arche à Lavertezzo TI
Ponte ad arco doppio presso Lavertezzo TI
Double-arched bridge near Lavertezzo TI

Seite 82: Corippo TI

Lavertezzo TI

Haus in Frasco TI
Maison à Frasco TI
Casa a Frasco TI
House in Frasco TI

Sonogno TI

Ronco TI

Ascona TI

Carona mit San Salvatore TI
Carona avec le San Salvatore TI
Carona con San Salvatore TI
Carona with the San Salvatore Mountain TI

Morcote TI

Gandria TI

Faszination Switzerland

Historisches und Aktuelles
Histoire et actualités
Storia e attualità
Past and present

Wissenswertes über die Schweiz

Un aperçu de la Suisse

Die Topographie unseres Landes

La topographie de notre pays

Die Schweiz ist, im Herzen Europas und an der Nahtstelle von drei seiner wichtigsten Kulturen und Sprachräume gelegen, nur ein an Ausdehnung kleines Land. Seine Fläche beträgt lediglich 41 293 km^2; von Ost nach West misst die grösste Distanz bloss 348 km, in Richtung Nord nach Süd sogar nur 220 km. Aber auf diesem knappen Raum ist eine Vielfältigkeit anzutreffen, die in der Welt ihresgleichen sucht. Das Territorium der Schweiz gliedert sich in die Alpen, die mehr als die Hälfte des Landes bedecken und sich bis auf einen Gipfelpunkt von 4634 m (Dufourspitze) erheben, in das flache bis leicht hügelige Mittelland, das sich vom Genfersee bis zum Bodensee erstreckt und ungefähr einen Drittel der Fläche einnimmt, sowie in den Jura (10%), der zum Teil aus einem Faltengebirge, zum Teil aus Höhenzügen mit weiten Tafeln besteht. Sowohl in den Alpen wie auch im Jura hat die Entwässerung eine grosse Zahl von tiefen Taleinschnitten bewirkt. Aus dem «Wasserschloss Schweiz» ergiessen sich Quellflüsse in vier Richtungen: in die Nordsee (Rhein mit dem Zufluss von Aare, Reuss und Limmat), ins Mittelmeer (Rhone), in die Adria (Tessin via Po) und in das Schwarze Meer (Inn via Donau).

La Suisse, située au cœur de l'Europe et au point de jonction de trois de ses cultures et régions linguistiques les plus importantes, n'est qu'un petit pays defaible étendue. Sa superficie n'est que de 41 293 km^2; de l'est à l'ouest, la plus grande distance est seulement de 348 km; du nord au sud, elle n'atteint que 220 km. Et pourtant sur cette étendue très limitée, on peut découvrir une diversité telle qu'elle n'a rien de pareil au monde. Le territoire de la Suisse se subdivise comme suit: les Alpes qui, à elles seules, couvrent plus de la moitié du pays et s'élèvent jusqu'à une altitude de 4634 m (Pointe Dufour); le Plateau, plat à légèrement vallonné, qui s'étend du lac Léman au lac de Constance et occupe environ un tiers du territoire; le Jura (10%), composé en partie de montagnes de plissement, de crêtes avec de vastes plateaux. Dans les Alpes comme dans le Jura, les eaux courantes sont à l'origine d'un grand nombre de vallées encaissées. En partant de ce «château d'eau» qu'est la Suisse, les cours d'eau s'écoulent dans quatre directions: vers la mer du Nord (le Rhin qui reçoit l'Aar, la Reuss et la Limmat), vers la Méditerranée (le Rhône), vers l'Adriatique (le Tessin via le Pô) et la mer Noire (l'Inn via le Danube).

Die Bevölkerung

La population

Die Mehrsprachigkeit der Schweiz

Le plurilinguisme de la Suisse

Die Topographie des Landes mit schneebedeckten Gipfeln, Gletschern, Felsformationen und vielen Seen führt dazu, dass ein grosser Teil der Landoberfläche nicht bewohnbar und kaum nutzbar ist. Das hat wiederum die Konzentration der zirka 6,9 Millionen umfassenden Bevölkerung auf einen eingeengten Raum zur Folge, so dass dieses Land praktisch eines der am dichtesten besiedelten nicht nur Europas, sondern auch der Welt ist. Auf diesem engen Raum werden nicht weniger als vier Sprachen in kompakten Gebieten gesprochen, nämlich von 74,4 Prozent ein in viele verschiedene Dialekte aufgesplittertes Deutsch, von 20,2 Prozent Französisch (im westlichen Teil des Landes), von 4,1 Prozent Italienisch (südlich der Alpen)

La topographie du pays - avec ses sommets enneigés, ses glaciers, ses formations rocheuses et ses nombreux lacs - a pour conséquence qu'une grande partie du pays n'est pas habitable et n'est guère utilisable de manière productive. Il en résulte que la population de 6,9 millions d'habitants environ est concentrée sur un espace restreint. Pratiquement, ce pays a donc l'une des densités de population parmi les plus élevées d'Europe, voire du monde. Sur cet espace restreint, on ne parle pas moins de quatre langues dans des régions compactes. 74,4% de la population parle une grande variété de dialectes allemands, 20,2% le français dans la partie occidentale du pays, 4,1% l'italien au sud des Alpes et 1%

Un compendio sulla Svizzera

Getting up to date on Switzerland

La topografia del nostro paese

The topography of our country

La Svizzera, situata nel cuore dell'Europa e al punto di congiunzione di tre delle sue culture e regioni linguistiche più importanti, non è che un piccolo paese di modesta estensione. La sua superficie è appena di 41 293 km^2; dall'est all'ovest, la più grande distanza è di 348 km soltanto; dal nord al sud, non raggiunge che i 220 km. E tuttavia, su questa estensione molto limitata, si può scoprire una diversità tale che non ha niente di simile al mondo. Il territorio della Svizzera si divide come segue: le Alpi che coprono da sole più della metà del paese e s'elevano fino a un'altitudine di 4634 m (Cima Dufour); il Mittelland (altopiano), piatto e leggermente collinoso, che s'estende dal lago di Ginevra fino al lago di Costanza e occupa circa un terzo del territorio; il Giura (10 %), che è costituita in parte da montagne di corrugamento, da creste con vasti altopiani. Nelle Alpi, come nel Giura, le acque correnti sono all'origine di un grande numero di vallate incassate. Partendo da questo «castello d'acqua» che è la Svizzera, i corsi d'acqua scorrono in quattro direzioni: verso il mare del Nord (il Reno con l'affluenza dell'Aare, la Reuss e la Limmat), verso il Mediterraneo (il Rodano), verso l'Adriatico (il Ticino via Po) e il Mar Nero (l'Inn via Danubio).

Switzerland lies in the heart of Europe at the crossroads of three of its most important cultural and language regions and is a relatively small country. Its land area consists only of 41,293 km^2 and measures at its greatest extent 348 km from East to West and from North to South only 220 km. Yet within this relatively small area a diversity of landscape is concentrated that is unique in the world. The territory encompassing Switzerland is divided into three topographical parts. The Alps cover more than half of the territory culminating in the highest point of the Monte Rosa at 4,634 m above sea level; the flat and slightly undulating Mittelland stretches from the Lake of Geneva to Lake Constance and takes up about one third of the territory; the Jura comprises around one tenth of the land mass partly made up of folded ranges and high outcrops with wide plateaux. Water drainage in the Alps and also in the Jura has cloven deep ravine valleys from the mountains. Four tributary rivers have their sources in the Swiss 'water reservoir'; the Aar, Reuss and Limmat flowing into the Rhine northwards to the North Sea; the Rhone westwards to the Mediterranean; the Ticino flowing into the Po towards the Adriatic, and the Inn flowing into the Danube to the Black Sea.

La popolazione

The population

Il plurilinguismo della Svizzera

Polyglot Switzerland

La topografia del paese - con le sue vette innevate, i suoi ghiacciai, le sue formazioni rocciose ed i suoi numerosi laghi - ha per conseguenza che una grande parte del paese non è abitabile e appena utilizzabile in modo produttivo. Di conseguenza, risulta che la popolazione di circa 6,9 milioni d'abitanti è concentrata su uno spazio ristretto. Questo paese ha dunque una delle densità di popolazione tra le più elevate non solo d'Europa, ma anche del mondo. Su questo spazio ristretto, si parla nientemeno che quattro lingue in regioni compatte. 74,4 % della popolazione parla una grande varietà di dialetti tedeschi, 20,2 % il francese nella parte occidentale del paese, 4,1% l'italiano

The topography of the country with snow capped peaks, glaciers, rock formations and many lakes makes much of the land area inhabitable and incapable of exploitation. This has the consequence of concentrating the population of 6.9 million into a restrictive area so that the population density in the inhabited part is not only the highest in Europe but also in the world as a whole. Within this restrictive area there are no less than four languages spoken in compact pockets of population. The German speakers account for 74.4%; but even these are split up into many different dialects of the Germanic tongue. In the West part of the country 20.2% speak French and in the South 4.1% have Italian

und von 1 Prozent Romanisch (im Alpenraum von Graubünden). Die ersteren drei Sprachen gelten als offizielle Nationalsprachen, die einander in jeder Beziehung gleichgestellt sind, während Romanisch als Landessprache anerkannt und vom Staat gefördert wird.

le romanche dans la région alpine des Grisons. Les trois premières langues sont les langues nationales officielles et sont mises sur un même pied d'égalité sous tous les rapports; le romanche, par contre, est reconnu langue du pays et est soutenu par l'Etat.

Die sprachliche, kulturelle, geographische Vielfalt und die politischen Strukturen

Les structures politiques et la diversité linguistique, culturelle et géographique

Die Schweiz ist von ihren geschichtlichen Anfängen ebenso wie von ihrer sprachlichen, kulturellen und geographischen Vielfalt her nicht zu einem Einheitsstaat mit zentralistisch ausgerichteten politischen Strukturen prädestiniert, sondern zu einem föderalistischen Muster des Staatsaufbaus, das den einzelstaatlichen Elementen (Kantone), ja sogar den rund 3000 Gemeinden ein unübliches Mass eigener Verantwortung und Kompetenzen belässt. So sind die 26 Kantone der Schweiz, die erst seit 1848 in einem Bundesstaat mit einer auch zentralen Regierung fest vereint sind, auch heute noch immer zuständig für die Polizei, für das Unterrichtswesen und für alle jene Bereiche, in denen nicht kraft Bundesverfassung dem Bund die Kompetenz übertragen worden ist. Der Föderalismus ist von alters her in der Mentalität der schweizerischen Bevölkerung sehr stark verwurzelt. Es war keineswegs leicht, in der modernen Schweiz jenes Mass von Zentralismus herbeizuführen, das in andern europäischen Staaten seit Jahrhunderten als Voraussetzung für die Führung eines effizienten Staatsapparats gegolten hat. Auch heute noch identifizieren sich die meisten Schweizer eher mit dem Kanton, dem sie herkunftsmässig als Bürger angehören, als mit der Nation. Erst in allerneuester Zeit hat die zunehmende Wanderung und Vermischung im Innern der Schweiz zu einer stärkeren Betonung der nationalen Identität gegenüber dem früheren Partikularismus geführt.

Du fait de ses débuts historiques, comme par suite de sa diversité linguistique, culturelle et géographique, la Suisse n'est pas prédestinée à être un Etat unitaire ayant des structures politiques à orientation centraliste. Elle est un Etat à modèle fédéraliste qui laisse à ses éléments individuels (les cantons), même aux 3000 communes, un degré tout à fait inhabituel de responsabilités et de compétences propres. C'est ainsi que les 26 cantons suisses, qui sont seulement réunis depuis 1848 en un Etat fédératif avec un gouvernement central, sont encore aujourd'hui compétents en matière de police, de scolarité et dans tous les domaines qui n'on pas été délégués à la Confédération sur la base de la Constitution fédérale. Depuis toujours, le fédéralisme est solidement enraciné dans la mentalité de la population suisse. Dans la Suisse moderne, il n'a pas du tout été facile d'en arriver à ce degré de centralisation qui est considéré, depuis des siècles, comme étant la condition requise à une direction efficace de l'appareil de l'Etat dans d'autres pays d'Europe. Même de nos jours, la conscience de l'identité nationale de la majorité des Suisses est restée celle de leur identification avec le canton dont ils sont citoyens du fait de leur origine. Ce n'est que très récemment que la migration et le brassage à l'intérieur de la Suisse ont mené à une accentuation de l'identité nationale comparativement au particularisme d'autrefois.

Die politischen Institutionen des schweizerischen Bundesstaates

Les institutions politiques de l'Etat fédéral

Die politischen Institutionen des schweizerischen Bundesstaates widerspiegeln getreulich diese föderalistische Komponente. Anlässlich der Gründung des Bundesstaates 1848 hat man sich für das bundesstaatliche Parlament zum Zwecke der Versöhnung des föderalistischen Elements mit den neuen, zentralistischen Notwendigkeiten einer effizienten Staatsführung den amerikanischen Kongress mit seinem Zweikammersystem zum Vorbild genommen: Der Nationalrat mit seiner auf der Bevölkerungszahl fussenden Bestellung der 200 Sitze entspricht dem ameri-

Les institutions politiques de la Confédération helvétique reflètent fidèlement ce composant fédéraliste. Lors de la fondation de l'Etat fédéral en 1848, on a pris exemple sur le Congrès américain et son bicaméralisme dans le but de concilier l'élément fédéraliste et les nécessités centralistes nouvelles d'une direction efficiente de l'Etat quand il a fallu mettre sur pied le parlement fédéral. Le Conseil national, dont la répartition des 200 sièges est fonction de la population, correspond à la Chambre des Représentants des Etats-Unis. Par contre, le Conseil des Etats avec

al sud delle Alpi e l'1 % il romancio nelle regioni alpine dei Grigioni. Le prime tre lingue sono le lingue nazionali ufficiali e sono messe sullo stesso piano d'uguaglianza in tutti i rapporti; il romancio, invece, è riconosciuta come lingua del paese e sostenuta dallo Stato.

as their mother tongue. In the Alpine Region of the Grisons 1% of the population speak Romanch. The first three languages are recognised federally as national languages and stand on equal footing to each other. Romanch is recognised as an ethnic medium of expression and is in fact encouraged and subsidised by the state.

La molteplicità linguistica, culturale, geografica e le strutture politiche

The linguistic, cultural, geographical variety and the political structures

Considerati i suoi inizi storici, nonché in seguito la sua diversità linguistica, culturale e geografica, la Svizzera non è predestinata ad essere uno Stato unitario con delle strutture politiche a orientamento centrale. Ella è un modello di federalismo che lascia ai suoi elementi individuali (i cantoni), come pure ai 3000 comuni, un livello piuttosto insolito di responsabilità e di competenza propria. È così che i 26 cantoni svizzeri, i quali sono riuniti dal 1848 in uno Stato federativo con un governo centrale, sono ancora oggi competenti in materia di polizia, scolarizzazione e in tutti i campi che non sono stati delegati alla Confederazione in base alla Costituzione federale. Da sempre, il federalismo è solidamente radicato nella mentalità della popolazione svizzera.
Nella Svizzera moderna, non è stato del tutto facile arrivare a questo grado di centralizzazione che è considerato, da secoli, come premessa a una direzione efficace dell'apparato dello Stato negli altri paesi d'Europa. Anche tuttora, la coscienza dell'identità nazionale della maggioranza degli Svizzeri è rimasta quella della loro identificazione con il cantone a cui appartengono effettivamente dalla nascita.
È solo di recente che l'emigrazione ed il mescolamento all'interno della Svizzera hanno portato a un'accentuazione dell'identità nazionale rispetto al particolarismo d'altri tempi.

Because of its diverse language, cultural and geographic structure as well as its historical origins Switzerland was not meant to become a monolithic state with centralised political institutions but rather to adopt a federalistic system of government which was to preserve independent single state units, the cantons, and within these around 3,000 political communities enjoying an unusual extent of political responsibility and competence. These 26 cantonal independent states which have been united since 1848 into a confederate national state-unit with a central federal government, are today still responsible for the police forces, for education and for all other government matters which have not been entrusted to the Confederation under the federal constitution. Federalism has been deeply rooted in the mentality of the Swiss population traditionally from early times. It was by no means easy to introduce in modern times into the Swiss state-form that extent of centralism which has been taken for granted in other European states for centuries as the precondition for the administration of an efficient political state apparatus. Even today the conscious national identity of the Swiss tends towards loyalty to the cantonal state to which they belong by virtue of origin as citizens. It was only in very recent times through increased migration and intermarriage among the population inside Switzerland that any strong emphasis upon a federal national identity was able to manifest itself against the early particularism.

Le istituzione politiche dello stato federale svizzero

The political institutions of the Swiss Confederation

Le istituzioni politiche della Confederazione elvetica riflettono fedelmente questi componenti federalisti. In occasione della fondazione dello Stato federale nel 1848, è stato preso come esempio il Congresso americano ed il suo bicameralismo allo scopo di conciliare l'elemento federalista e le nuove necessità accentrati d'una direzione efficente dello Stato quando si è dovuto creare il parlamento federale. Il Consiglio nazionale, la cui ripartizione dei

The political institutions of the Swiss Confederate State reflect precisely such federalistic components. When the Confederate State was founded in 1848 the example of the American Congress with its bicameral system was followed in creating a Confederate State Parliament with the objective of compensating for the new centralistic necessity of an efficient supranational government with the federalistic ideals of cantonal independence. The

kanischen Repräsentantenhaus, während der Ständerat mit 46 Sitzen (zwei pro Kanton) für die politische Repräsentation der Einzelstaaten im Bund sorgt, wie das in Amerika die Rolle des Senats ist.

Gemeinsam bilden Nationalrat und Ständerat die Bundesversammlung, das oberste Organ der Eidgenossenschaft. Sie ist für die allerwichtigsten Entscheide zuständig, so etwa die Wahl der Regierungsmitglieder (Bundesrat). Eine Eigenheit des politischen Systems der Schweiz ist es, dass es im eigentlichen Sinn keinen Staatspräsidenten und auch keinen Ministerpräsidenten kennt, der einem Kabinett von Fachministern vorsteht. Vielmehr ist in der Schweiz auf der Regierungsebene ein Kollegium von sieben einander gleichgestellten Bundesräten tätig, von denen ein jeder durch die Bundesversammlung als Regierungsmitglied gewählt worden ist. Sie verteilen untereinander die Ressorts. Die Regierungsentscheide werden von dieser Kollegialbehörde mit Mehrheitsentscheid getroffen, wobei jeweilen für ein Jahr einer der sieben Bundesräte entsprechend einem Turnus den Vorsitz führt. Der Präsident des Bundesrats trägt den Titel eines Bundespräsidenten, was ihn zur Staatsrepräsentation legitimiert. Die Bundesräte gehören den wichtigsten Parteien, wie sie im Parlament vertreten sind, an; es wird Sorge getragen, dass die einzelnen Sprachgruppen und Kulturen sowie die beiden Konfessionen (Protestanten und Katholiken) und die verschiedenen Regionen des Landes in der Regierung mehr oder weniger angemessen vertreten sind.

Eine typisch schweizerische Errungenschaft: die direkte Demokratie

Eine typisch schweizerische Errungenschaft ist die Ausbildung der sogenannten direkten Demokratie, die darin besteht, dass die Stimmbürger nicht nur zu periodischen Parlamentswahlen aufgerufen werden oder bisweilen in einem Referendum eine Sachfrage entscheiden sollen, sondern dass mit 50 000 gesammelten Unterschriften jedes vom Parlament verabschiedete Gesetz einem Volksentscheid unterstellt werden kann; mit einer Volksinitiative, die von 100 000 Bürgern unterstützt wird, kann sogar eine Verfassungsänderung bewirkt werden, wenn in der betreffenden Volksabstimmung das Volksmehr und eine Mehrheit der Kantone aus den Urnen hervorgeht.

ses 46 sièges (deux par canton) assure la représentation politique des Etats individuels dans la Confédération, comme c'est le rôle du Sénat aux Etats-Unis.

Le Conseil national et le Conseil des Etats forment ensemble l'Assemblée fédérale, organe suprême de la Confédération. Elle est compétente pour les décisions les plus importantes, par exemple l'élection des membres du gouvernement (Conseil fédéral). Une des particulantés du système politique suisse est de ne pas avoir, dans le sens proprement dit, de président de l'Etat, ni de président du Conseil des ministres qui dirigerait un cabinet de ministres compétents.
Au niveau gouvernemental suisse, un collège de sept conseillers fédéraux qui sont sur un pied d'égalité exerce son activité; chacun des conseillers a été élu membre du gouvernement par l'Assemblée fédérale. Ils répartissent entre eux les différents ressorts. Les décisions gouvernementales sont prises à la majorité par ce collège, un des sept conseillers fédéraux assumant la présidence à tour de rôle pour un an. Le président du Conseil fédéral porte le titre de président de la Confédération, titre qui le légitime à la représentation de l'Etat. Les conseillers fédéraux appartiennent aux partis les plus importants représentés au Parlement. On prend également soin que les différents groupes linguistiques et les cultures, les deux confessions (protestants et catholiques) et les différentes régions du pays soient représentés plus ou moins équitablement au sein du gouvernement.

Une particularité helvétique: la démocratie directe

L'une des conquêtes typiquement suisses est l'existence de la démocratie directe. En plus du fait que les électeurs soient appelés à l'élection périodique du Parlement ou à décider de temps à autre d'un objet par référendum, cette démocratie directe consiste à pouvoir soumettre, moyennant 50 000 signatures récoltés, toute loi adoptée par le Parlement à revotation populaire. Au moyen d'une initiative populaire, soutenue par 100 000 citoyens, il est même possible d'obtenir une modification de la Constitution pour autant que, lors de la votation correspondante, on obtienne la majorité du peuple et celle des cantons.

200 seggi è compito della popolazione, corrisponde alla Camera dei Rappresentanti degli Stati Uniti. Invece, il Consiglio degli Stati con i suoi 46 seggi (due per cantone) assicura la rappresentazione politica degli Stati individuali nella Confederazione, come è il ruolo del Senato negli Stati Uniti.

Il Consiglio nazionale e il Consiglio degli Stati formano insieme l'Assemblea federale, organo supremo della Confederazione. Essa è competente per le decisioni più importanti, per esempio l'elezione dei membri del governo (Consiglio federale). Una delle particolarità del sistema politico svizzero è di non avere, nel vero senso della parola, né un presidente di stato, né un presidente del Consiglio dei ministri che dirigerebbero un cabinetto di ministri competenti. A livello governativo svizzero, un collegio di sette consiglieri federali, messi allo stesso livello, esercita la sua attività; ognuno dei consiglieri è stato eletto membro del governo dall'Assemblea federale. Si dividono tra di loro i differenti ressorts. Le decisioni governative sono prese in maggioranza da questo collegio, uno dei sette consiglieri federali assumendo la presidenza a turno per la durata d'un anno. Il presidente del Consiglio federale porta il titolo di presidente della Confederazione, titolo che lo leggittima a rappresentare lo Stato. I consiglieri federali appartengono ai partiti più importanti rappresentati al Parlamento. Si tiene conto ugualmente che i differenti gruppi linguistici e le culture, le due confessioni (protestante e cattolica) e le differenti regioni del paese siano rappresentati più o meno imparzialmente nel seno del governo.

National Council having 200 representatives based on the number of population is equivalent to the American House of Representatives whilst the Council of the States having 46 seats (two per canton) takes care of the political representation of the single states within the Confederation; it has therefore the same function as the American Senate.

Together the National Council and the Council of States form the Federal Assembly which is the highest political body of the Confederation. The Federal Assembly is competent to take decisions on the most important matters as for example the election of the members of government, the Federal Council. It is a unique characteristic of the Swiss political system that there is in fact no state president and no prime minister with a cabinet of ministers subordinate to him. The government level in Switzerland consists rather of a team of seven equal Federal Councillors each elected as a member of government by the Federal Assembly. The various departments of state are distributed among these seven Federal Councillors. Government decisions are taken within this collegiate authority by a majority of votes, and one of the Federal Councillors takes the chair in council for one year only on a rotation system. The Chairman of the Federal Council is vested with the title of President of the Confederation giving him the status of head of state. The Federal Councillors are drawn from the more important political parties as represented in parliament as a whole, and much care is taken to see that the various language groups and cultures as well as the two church denominations of protestant and Roman Catholic and the various regions of the country are more or less appropriately represented in the government.

Una tipica conquista svizzera: la democrazia diretta

Una delle conquiste tipicamente svizzere è l'esistenza della democrazia diretta che consiste nel fatto che gli elettori siano chiamati alle urne periodicamente per l'elezione periodica del Parlamento o per decidere di tanto in tanto d'una questione specifica per mezzo del referendum. Questa democrazia diretta consiste nel poter sottomettere mediante 50 000 firme raccolte qualsiasi legge adottata dal Parlamento a una votazione popolare. Tramite un'iniziativa popolare, sostenuta da 100 000 cittadini, è pure possibile

A typical Swiss achievement: Direct democracy

A typical feature of the Swiss political system is the development of the 'direct democracy' which consists not only of calling out voters for periodical parliamentary elections or for occasional plebiscites on various technical questions, but also manifests itself in the fact that all acts of parliament upon the statute book can be made subject to the final decision of a plebiscite by collecting 50,000 signatures among the population to enforce this. A political initiative supported by 100,000 signatures can even demand a change

Ein kurzer Abriss der Geschichte

Un bref rappel historique

Nun noch ein kurzer Abriss der Geschichte: Die Schweiz war um 800 Bestandteil des Reiches von Karl dem Grossen und gelangte nach der Aufteilung des fränkischen Imperiums zum ostfränkischen Teilreich (Deutschland). Aus dieser Zugehörigkeit löste sich die Schweiz im späten Mittelalter mit einer wachsenden Zahl von reichsabtrünnigen Kantonen in einem vielhundertjährigen Prozess nach und nach los. Uri, Schwyz und Unterwalden gaben mit dem legendären Schwur der «Eidgenossen» auf dem Rütli und einem denkwürdigen Bundesbrief von 1291 die Initialzündung. Die alten Schweizer schlugen sich auf allen Schlachtfeldern hervorragend, zuerst im Kampf gegen die Habsburger, später auch gegen das aufstrebende Burgund unter Karl dem Kühnen sowie gegen den deutschen Kaiser Maximilian (1499).

Für kurze Zeit spielte damals die so siegreiche Eidgenossenschaft eine aktive Rolle in der europäischen Machtpolitik, bis ihren Truppen 1515 bei Marignano (Po-Ebene) vom französischen König Franz I. und dessen venezianischen Bundesgenossen eine schwere Niederlage beschert wurde. Fortan befleissigte sich der schweizerische Staatenbund der Neutralität und verhielt sich innerhalb seiner damaligen Grenzen still. Die alte Eidgenossenschaft fand 1798 ihr Ende durch Napoleon, der die Schweiz militärisch eroberte und sie Frankreich botmässig machte.

Die Zeit nach 1815 (Wiener Kongress) war geprägt durch Versuche, der vom napoleonischen Joch befreiten Schweiz eine den modernen Anforderungen gemässe einheitlichere Staatsform zu verschaffen, was aber erst 1848 – und nicht ohne einen kurzen, konfessionell gefärbten Bürgerkrieg – auf Grund des definitiven Übergangs zu einem neu strukturierten Bundesstaat mit den Kantonen übergeordneter Zentralgewalt schliesslich gelang. Seither hat die Schweiz sich mit ihrer bewaffneten Neutralität eines dauernden Friedens erfreut und einen spektakulären Aufstieg von einem vormals armen Agrarstaat zu einem modernen Industriestaat mit grossem Wohlstand durchgemacht.

Pour terminer, voici encore un sommaire historique. Aux environs de l'an 800, la Suisse faisait partie de l'empire de Charlemagne. Après le partage de l'empire des Francs, elle a été intégrée à la partie des Francs orientaux (Allemagne). La Suisse s'est détachée peu à peu de cette appartenance à la fin du Moyen Age - nombre croissant de cantons renégats - au cours d'un processus qui s'est étalé sur des siècles. L'amorçage initial a été le fait d'Uri de Schwyz et d 'Unterwald: le serment légendaire des «Confédérés» au Rütli et le mémorable pacte de confédération de 1291. Les anciens suisses se sont comportés vaillamment sur tous les champs de bataille; d'abord au cours de la lutte contre les Habsbourg, plus tard contre la Bourgogne en plein développement sous Charles le Téméraire et ensuite contre l'empereur d'Allemagne Maximilian (1499).

Pour peu de temps, la Confédération, si victorieuse à cette époque, a joué un rôle actif dans la politique de puissance européenne jusqu'au moment où ses troupes ont subi une lourde défaite en 1515 près de Marignan (plaine du Pô), défaite infligée par le roi de France François Ier et ses alliés vénitiens. Par la suite, la Confédération d'Etats suisses s'est évertuée à rester neutre et à se tenir tranquille à l'intérieur des frontières de l'époque. C'est par Napoléon que l'ancienne Confédération a connu sa fin en 1798. L'empereur l'a conquise militairement et l'a soumise à la France.

Les temps après 1815 (Congrès de Vienne) ont été empreintes de tentatives visant à donner au pays libéré du joug de Napoléon un système gouvernemental plus homogène et répondant aux nécessités modernes. Cependant, on n'y est parvenu qu'en 1848 - et non sans une courte guerre civile teintée de questions confessionnelles - en passant définitivement à un Etat confédéré structuré ayant un pouvoir central coiffant les cantons. Depuis lors, la Suisse a pu se réjouir d'une paix continuelle avec sa neutralité armée. Elle a connu une croissance spectaculaire, passant de l'état d'un pays agricole pauvre à celui d'une nation industrielle à grande prospérité.

Die Schweiz ist ein Land ohne nennenswerte Bodenschätze

La Suisse est un pays sans richesses naturelles particulières du sous-sol

Die Schweiz ist ein Land ohne nennenswerte Bodenschätze. Wenn man einmal von der Land- und Forstwirtschaft sowie von der Wasserkraft absieht, ist nichts an

La Suisse est un pays qui ne possède guère de richesses naturelles dans son sous-sol. Si on fait abstraction de l'économie agricole et forestière ainsi que du

ottenere una modifica della Costituzione, qualora nella corrispondente votazione, si ottenga la maggioranza del popolo e quella dei cantoni.

in the Constitution and such can be effected by a majority of votes in a plebiscite provided that a majority of the cantons as represented by the origin of the votes cast also exists at the same time.

Un breve schizzo della Svizzera

A short summary of the history

Per terminare, ecco un riassunto storico. Agli inizi dell'anno 800, la Svizzera faceva parte dell'impero di Carlomagno. Dopo la divisione dell'impero dei Franchi, ella è stata integrata nella parte dei Franchi orientali (Germania). La Svizzera, si è distaccata a poco a poco da questa appartenenza alla fine del Medio Evo - numero crescente di cantoni rinnegati - nel corso di un processo della durata di secoli. La carica d'innesco è stato l'atto di Uri, di Schwyz e di Unterwald: il giuramento leggendario dei «Confederati» al Rütli e il memorabile patto di confederazione del 1291. Gli antenati svizzeri si sono comportati valorosamente su tutti i campi di battaglia; dapprima nel corso della lotta contro gli Asburgo, più tardi contro i Borgogna in pieno sviluppo sotto Carlo il Temerario ed in seguito contro l'imperatore di Germania Massimiliano (1499).

As a conclusion a short resume of Swiss history: around 800 AD the territory which is now Switzerland was part of the Empire of Charlemagne and after the dissolution of the Frankish Realm became part of the Eastern Frankish Empire now known as Germany. Switzerland emerged from its membership of this sphere of influence little by little over some hundreds of years commencing in the later Middle Ages when an increasing number of cantonal states defected from the imperial yoke. The initial flame of the yearning for independence was kindled on the Rutli Meadow with the legendary oath of the original confederates of the Cantons of Uri, Schwyz and Unterwalden formally documented in the memorable Confederate Charter signed in 1291. The ancient Swiss gave excellent acounts of themselves on all fields of battle, first in their struggle against the Hapsburgs and later against the ambitious power of the Dukes of Burgundy under Charles the Bold as well as later in 1499 beating the armies of the German Emperor Maximillian.

Per poco tempo, la Confederazione, così vittoriosa a quell'epoca, ha avuto un ruolo attivo nella politica di potere europea fino al momento quando le sue truppe hanno subito una dura sconfitta nel 1515 presso Marignano (pianura padana), sconfitta inflitta dal re di Francia Francesco 1° e i suoi alleati veneziani. In seguito, la Confederazione dello Stato svizzero si è sforzata a restare neutrale e di tenersi tranquilla entro le frontiere d'allora. L'antica Confederazione ha conosciuto la sua fine nel 1798 a causa di Napoleone. L'imperatore l'ha conquistata militarmente e l'ha sottomessa alla Francia.

For a short period the then victorious Confederation played an active role in European power politics until its forces were severly defeated in 1515 at the Battle of Marignano in the Po Valley by the French monarch Charles I and his Venetian allies. From that time onwards the Swiss Federated States kept themselves strictly neutral and remained passively within their own boundaries. An end was put to the old Confederation in 1798 by Napoleon who subjected it militarily and politically.

I tempi dopo il 1815 (Congresso di Vienna) sono stati improntati da tentativi miranti a donare al paese, liberato dal giogo di Napoleone, un sistema di governo più omogeneo e corrispondente alle esigenze moderne. Tuttavia, si è raggiunto ciò non prima del 1848 - e non senza una breve guerra civile improntata da questioni confessionali - passando definitivamente a uno Stato confederato strutturato avente

The period from 1815, the year of the Congress of Vienna, was distinguished by attempting the conversion of liberated Switzerland into a more unitarian form of state appropriate to the modern requirements of the day after the relinquishment of the Napoleonic hegemony; this was only finally successful in 1848, after a short religiously-coloured period of civil war, on the basis of a definite transition

primären Ressourcen vorhanden, was den Lebensunterhalt der Bevölkerung aus dem eigenen Boden gewährleisten könnte. Aus dieser Kärglichkeit der Natur entsprang die Notwendigkeit, das wirtschaftliche Auskommen mit im Ausland vermarktbaren Arbeits- und Dienstleistungen zu suchen. Die Rohstoffe werden zur Verarbeitung importiert, worauf die Produkte des Veredelungsprozesses grossenteils wieder exportiert werden. Der Erlös aus der Wertsteigerung stellt zu einem guten Teil die ökonomische Existenzgrundlage der Schweiz dar, zumal in normalen Zeiten etwa die Hälfte aller Nahrungsmittel und sämtliche fossilen Energieträger ebenfalls aus dem Ausland bezogen werden müssen. Die Bedeutung des Aussenhandels für die Schweiz geht daraus bildhaft hervor, dass praktisch jeder dritte in der Schweiz verdiente Franken aus dem Export von Waren oder Dienstleistungen stammt. Dennoch ist die Handelsbilanz der Schweiz negativ. Wenn demgegenüber aber die Ertragsbilanz einen namhaften Überschuss aufweist, so ist das auf den positiven Saldo der Kapitalgewinne, des Tourismus und anderer «unsichtbarer Transaktionen» zurückzuführen.

Der Aufstieg der Schweiz in die Spitzengruppe der Länder mit dem höchsten Lebensstandard hat seine Wurzeln gewiss in einer Reihe von günstigen Konstellationen, aber eben auch darin, dass die Schweizer im Durchschnitt arbeitswillig, gründlich, qualitätsbewusst, sparsam und riskanten Experimenten und emotionalen Exzessen abhold sind. Die politischen und gesetzlichen Rahmenbedingungen für eine erfolgreiche wirtschaftliche Tätigkeit sind, wennschon die Belastung mit Steuern und Sozialabgaben auch in der Schweiz bereits bedrohlich zugenommen hat, verhältnismässig günstig geblieben: Die private Initiative kann sich immer noch als kräftiger Impuls des Wachstums der Wirtschaft auswirken. Protektionistische Massnahmen des Staats werden – ausser im Bereich der agrarischen Produktion – in der Regel strikte abgelehnt.

Während die Landwirtschaft an Zahl der Beschäftigten (heute noch zirka 6%), nicht aber in bezug auf ihre Produktivität zurückgeht, sind Industrie und Gewerbe immer stärker geworden. Im industriellen Bereich

potentiel hydraulique, il n'y a rien comme ressources primaires qui puisse assurer la subsistance de la population en partant du propre sol. C'est de cette avarice de la nature qu'est issue la nécessité de rechercher la survie économique au moyen de la commercialisation à l'étranger de prestations de travaux et de services. Les matières premières sont importées en vue de leur transformation et, après le processus d'ennoblissement, les produits sont réexportés en grande partie. Les revenus tirés de cette plus-value représentent pour une bonne partie la base d'existence économique de la Suisse, d'autant plus qu'en temps normal environ la moitié de tous les produits alimentaires ainsi que toutes les énergies fossiles doivent également être importés de l'étranger. L'importance du commerce extérieur de la Suisse est illustrée par le fait que pratiquement un franc sur trois gagné en Suisse provient d'exportations de marchandise ou de prestations de services. Malgré cela, la balance commerciale de la Suisse est négative. Si, comparativement à cela, le solde de l'exploitation présente un excédent remarquable, c'est grâce au solde positif des bénéfices en capitaux, au tourisme et à d'autres «transactions invisibles».

Si la Suisse a réalisé son ascension dans le groupe des pays disposant du standard de vie le plus élevé, les raisons doivent certainement être recherchées dans une série de constellations favorables, mais également dans le fait qu'en général les Suisses ont la volonté de travailler, sont minutieux, aiment ce qui est de qualité, sont économes et hostiles aux expériences risquées comme aux excès à caractère émotionnel. Bien que la charge fiscale et les charges sociales se soient aussi accrues de manière menaçante en Suisse, les conditions politiques et légales n'en sont pas moins restées relativement favorables. L'initiative privée peut encore toujours se répercuter positivement et donner des impulsions en vue de la croissance économique. A l'exception de la production agricole, toutes les mesures protectionnistes de l'Etat sont rejetées strictement.

Tandis que l'agriculture est en recul du point de vue des personnes employées (maintenant encore 6%) mais non en ce qui concerne la productivité, l'industrie et les métiers n'ont cessé de gagner en puis-

Die Bedeutung des Aussenhandels für die Schweiz

L'importance du commerce extérieur pour la Suisse

Die Landwirtschaft, die Industrie und das Gewerbe

L'agriculture, l'industrie et l'artisanat

un potere centrale sui cantoni. D'allora, la Svizzera ha potuto godere di una pace continua con la sua neutralità armata. Essa ha conosciuto una crescita spettacolare, passando dalla condizione di paese agricolo povero a quella di una nazione industrializzata di grande prosperità.

to a newly structured Confederate state-form with the cantonal states now subordinate to a central authority. Since that time Switzerland has continued to enjoy lasting peace with its policy of armed neutrality and has achieved a spectacular growth from its humble origins of an impoverished agrarian state community to the stature of a modern industrial state with great prosperity unequalled anywhere.

La Svizzera è un paese senza rilevanti ricchezze del sottosuolo

Switzerland is a country without any mineral resources worth mentioning

La Svizzera è un paese che non possiede alcuna ricchezza naturale del sottosuolo. Se si fa eccezione dell'economia agricola e forestale così come del potenziale idraulico, non ci sono risorse primarie che potessero assicurare il sostentamento della popolazione partendo dal proprio suolo. È a causa di questa avaria della natura che è insorta la necessità di ricercare la sopravvivenza economica tramite la commercializzazione all'estero delle prestazioni di lavoro e di servizio. Le materie prime sono importati per la loro trasformazione e, dopo il processo di trasformazione, i prodotti sono in gran parte riesportati. Gli introiti ricavati da questo aumento di valore rappresenta per una buona parte la base d'esistenza economica della Svizzera, tanto più che in tempi normali circa la metà di tutti i prodotti alimentari così come di tutte le energie fossili debbano ugualmente essere importate dall'estero. L'importanza del commercio estero della Svizzera è dimostrato chiaramente dal fatto che praticamente un franco su tre guadagnato in Svizzera proviene da esportazioni di merci o da prestazioni di servizio. Malgrado ciò, il bilancio commerciale della Svizzera è negativo. Se, però rispetto a ciò il saldo dei profitti presenta una notevole eccedenza, è grazie al saldo positivo dei benefici in capitali, al turismo e ad altre «transazioni invisibili».

Switzerland is a country lacking in any mineral resources worth mentioning. Apart from agriculture and forestry as well as hydropower there are no primary resources whatsoever available that could guarantee a living to the native population from their own ground. Such barrenness of nature gave rise to the necessity of seeking to further the economic existence of the nation in the marketing of services and labour-intensive industries abroad. Raw materials are imported for processing and then the resulting products emanating from such finishing work are largely re-exported. The returns from such creation of wealth represent to a large extent the economic existential foundation of the Swiss population. It should be remembered that in normal times approximately half of all foodstuffs and all fossil fuels have to be imported from abroad. The significance of foreign trade for Switzerland can best be pictured by the fact that practically every third Swiss Franc earned stems from the exportation of goods or services. The balance of trade nevertheless is negative. If the over-all balance shows a considerable surplus, this is due to a positive balance in capital gains, tourism and other invisible earnings.

L'importanza del commercio con l'estero per la Svizzera

The significance of foreign trade for Switzerland

Se la Svizzera ha realizzato la sua ascesa nel gruppo dei paesi disponendo del più elevato standard di vita, le ragioni devono certamente essere ricercate in una serie di costellazioni favorevoli, ma è da attribuire anche al fatto che in generale gli Svizzeri hanno la volontà di lavorare, sono minuziosi, amano la qualità, sono risparmiatori e ostili alle esperienze rischiose come ad un eccesso di carattere emozionale. Nonostante gli oneri fiscali e sociali siano aumentati in Svizzera già in maniera minacciosa, le condizioni politiche e legali sono rimaste relativamente favorevoli.

The accession of Switzerland to the top group of those countries enjoying the highest standards of living certainly has its roots in a series of favourable constellations; but it can also be explained by the fact that the average Swiss is industrious, conscientious, quality conscious, thrifty and averse to risky experiments and emotional excesses. The political and statutory background conditions for successful economic activity have remained relatively favourable, although taxation and social security deductions have begun to take on threatening proportions in Switzerland

steht die Metall- und Maschinenindustrie an der Spitze; sie bestreitet fast die Hälfte aller Exporte. Von Weltbedeutung ist die chemische Industrie, die sich im Pharma- und Farbstoffbereich besonders hervortut. Traditionell ist die Schweiz auch ein Weltzentrum der Uhrenindustrie.
Von alters her war die Schweiz auch ein Land mit viel Textilindustrie. Diese hat aber heute unter dem Druck fernöstlicher Konkurrenz einen eher schweren Stand. Berühmt ist auch der Schweizer Käse, von dessen Produktion jährlich knapp die Hälfte exportiert wird.

sance. Dans le secteur industriel, c'est l'industrie des métaux et des machines qui vient en tête; elle est pratiquement à l'origine de la moitié des exportations. L'industrie chimique est également d'importance mondiale et se distingue notamment dans les domaines de la pharmacie et des matières colorantes. C'est par tradition que la Suisse est un centre mondial de l'industrie horlogère. De tout temps, la Suisse a été un pays ayant beaucoup d'industrie textile. Mais, à l'heure actuelle, celle-ci se trouve dans une position plutôt difficile sous la pression de la concurrence d'Extrême-Orient. Le fromage suisse est renommé lui aussi; presque la moitié de la production est exportée chaque année.

Der Dienstleistungsbereich

Le secteur des services

Im Dienstleistungsbereich haben die Banken und Versicherungen ein sprunghaftes Wachstum erlebt. Der aufstrebende «Finanzplatz Schweiz» ist längst in aller Mund; dessen Erfolge haben natürlich auch Neider auf den Plan gerufen, die vor allem das in der Schweiz strikte eingehaltene Bankgeheimnis verketzern möchten. In Wirklichkeit bietet dieses aber keinen Schutz gegen Delikte des ordentlichen Strafrechts.

Dans le domaine des prestations de services, les banques et compagnies d'assurance ont connu une croissance par bonds. Depuis longtemps, tout le monde parle de la «Place financière suisse» dont les succès ont, bien entendu, vu naître bien des envieux. Ceux-ci voudraient surtout discréditer le secret bancaire qui est observé strictement. En réalité, celui-ci n'offre pas de protection contre les délits de droit commun.

Die Medien

Les médias

Die Schweiz ist ein medienintensives Land. Es gibt eine Zeitung auf 50 000 Einwohner, doppelt soviel wie in den USA, zehnmal soviel wie in Deutschland und fünfzehnmal soviel wie in Italien. Insgesamt sind es gegen 200 in deutscher Sprache, 70 in französischer Sprache und etwa ein Dutzend in italienischer Sprache. Dazu kommen ein paar Titel in Rumantsch, der vierten Landessprache. Ebenso vielfältig wie bei den Printmedien ist das Angebot im Bereich der elektronischen Medien. Die Schweizerische Radio- und Fernsehgesellschaft SRG produziert für den nationalen Bedarf in zehn Studios neun Programme. Dazu kommt das Angebot von etwa drei Dutzend Privatradios. In jeder Sprachregion unterhält die SRG ein eigenes TV-Studio.

La Suisse est le pays des médias par excellence. On y compte un journal pour 50 000 habitants, soit deux fois plus qu'aux Etats-Unis, dix fois plus qu'en Allemagne et quinze fois plus qu'en Italie. Cela représente près de 200 publications en langue allemande, 70 en français et une douzaine en italien, plus quelques titres en romanche, quatrième langue nationale. Même diversité dans les médias électroniques. La SSR, Société suisse de Radiodiffusion et Télévision, produit, pour les besoins du pays, neuf programmes dans dix studios. A quoi il faut ajouter les émissions de plus d'une trentaine de radios privées. La SSR dispose, dans chaque région linguistique, de ses propres studios de télévision.

Die Schweiz gehört zu den meistverkabelten Ländern der Welt. Mehrere hundert private Kabelnetzbetreiber verbreiten lokal und regional schweizerische und ausländische Radio- und Fernsehprogramme. Während Jahrzehnten war Schweizer Radio International SRI – das internationale Programm der SRG – das einzige im Ausland wirksame Medium. Heute ist die

La Suisse est un des pays les plus câblés du monde. Plusieurs centaines d'exploitants de ces réseaux diffusent des programmes de radio et de télévision locaux, régionaux et étrangers. Pendant plusieurs années, la RSI, Radio Suisse Internationale - programme international de la SSR -, fut le seul média suisse actif à l'étranger. Aujourd'hui, la SSR figure dans

L'iniziativa privata può ancora sempre ripercuotersi positivamente e dare degli impulsi in vista della crescita economica. Ad eccezione della produzione agricola, tutte le misure di protezione dello Stato sono rigorosamente rifiutate.

too; but nevertheless private initiative is still able to manifest itself as an active impulse in economic growth. Protectionist measures by the state are, as a rule, deprecated, except in the area of agricultural production.

L'agricoltura, l'industria media

Mentre l'agricoltura è in regresso dal punto di vista delle persone impiegate (attualmente 6 %) ma non per quanto concerne la produttività, l'industria ed i mestieri non hanno cessato di guadagnare in potenza. Nel settore industriale, è l'industria metallurgica e delle macchine in testa; essa è praticamente all'origine della metà delle esportazioni. L'industria chimica è ugualmente d'importanza mondiale e si distingue enormemente nel campo farmaceutico e delle materie coloranti. Per tradizione la Svizzera è un centro mondiale dell'industria orologiera. Da sempre, la Svizzera è stata un paese avente molta industria tessile. Ma, attualmente, questo ramo si trova in una posizione piuttosto difficile essendo sotto la pressione della concorrenza dell'Estremo Oriente. Anche il formaggio svizzero è rinomato; quasi la metà della produzione è esportata ogni anno.

Agriculture, industry and the trades

Whilst agricultural production remains constant the number of persons engaged therein continues to fall, at present about 6% of the working population. In the case of trade and industry, however, production is constantly increasing. The metalworking and engineering industries stand at the top of the list in the manufacturing sector and provide almost half of all exports. The chemical industry is of great importance and world renowned for its pharmaceutical and dyestuff products. Traditionally Switzerland has been the world centre of the watchmaking industry. From early times Switzerland has also been a country with a large textile industry; this sector has a difficult task defending itself against the competition from the Far East. Swiss cheeses are also world famous; half the production here is exported.

Il settore terziario

Nel campo delle prestazioni di servizio, le banche e le compagnie d'assicurazioni hanno avuto una crescita a sbalzi. Da tanto tempo, tutto il mondo parla della «Piazza finanziaria svizzera» il cui successo ha, ben inteso, visto nascere molti invidiosi, i quali vorrebbero soprattutto discreditare il segreto bancario, rigorosamente mantenuto. In realtà, quest'ultimo non offre la protezione contro i delitti di diritto comune.

The service sector

The service industries of banking and insurance have experienced growth by leaps and bounds. The up-and-coming Swiss Finance Market is on the tip of every tongue and its successes have, of course, generated grudging acclaim principally expressed in invective against the strictly observed bank secrecy. In fact such discretion offers absolutely no protection against transgressions of Swiss criminal law.

I massmèdia

La Svizzera è un Paese dotato di intensive massmèdia. Esiste una redazione di giornale per ogni 50 000 abitanti; il doppio degli Stati Uniti, dieci volte di più della Germania e quindici volte di più dell'Italia. Nell'insieme sono circa 200 di lingua tedesca, 70 di lingua francese ed una dozzina di lingua italiana. Inoltre, un paio di titoli in romancio, la quarta lingua nazionale. L'offerta nel campo dei mèdia dell'elettronica è ugualmente varia come per le printmèdia. La Società Svizzera di Radiodiffusione e Televisione SSR trasmette per il fabbisogno nazionale nove programmi in dieci studi. Inoltre, è da aggiungere l'offerta di circa tre dozzine di radio private. In ogni regione linguistica la SSR ha un proprio studio TV.

The media

Switzerland is a country rich in media. There is one newspaper for every 50,000 inhabitants; twice as many as in the USA, ten times as many as in Germany and fifteen times as many as in Italy. In total there are around 200 in German, 70 in French and a dozen in Italian language. There are also a few in Rhaeto-Romanch, the fourth national language. Equally diversified as the printed media are the electronic media. The Swiss Radio and Television Company (SRG) produces nine programs in ten studios for domestic requirements. In addition there are three dozen private radio stations. SRG operates a TV studio in each language region.

SRG in vielen europäischen Satellitenprogrammen vertreten. SRI sendet weltweit via Kurzwelle und europaweit via Satellit ASTRA. Über 700 Stationen übernehmen seine Musik- und Dokumentarprogramme. In der Schweiz bietet SRI via Kabel mehrsprachige Programme für ausländische Gäste sowie Nachrichten in Englisch.

de nombreux programmes européens diffusés par satellites. La RSI est présente en Europe et dans le monde grâce au satellite ASTRA pour ondes courtes. Plus de 700 stations captent ses émissions. La RSI diffuse en Suisse, par câble, un programme multilingue pour les étrangers, ainsi que des nouvelles en anglais.

Die Stellung der Schweiz als Ferien- und Reiseland

La situation de la Suisse en tant que pays de vacances et de voyage

Wegen ihrer geographischen Lage war die Schweiz von jeher zum Transitland prädestiniert. Insbesondere durchquerten schon früh viele Reisende das Land über die Alpenpässe. Im Zeichen des aufkommenden Ferien- und Sporttourismus trugen die einzigartigen Naturschönheiten viel zur Entwicklung des Fremdenverkehrs bei. Heute ist eine überaus vielfältige Infrastruktur der Verkehrswege, der Beherbergung und der touristischen Attraktionen für Erholung und Kuraufenthalte sowie für Sommer- und Wintersport vorhanden. Viele Fremdenorte und städtische Zentren der Schweiz geniessen Weltruf. Aber nicht nur erstrangige Hotels und Gaststätten mit exquisiter Küche verwöhnen hier die anspruchsvollen Gäste, sondern auch einfache und billigere Fazilitäten ermöglichen Leuten mit beschränkteren Mitteln einen angenehmen Ferienaufenthalt. Weil hier im allgemeinen nach wie vor für gutes Geld auch ein guter Gegenwert an Dienstleistungen geboten wird, ist die Stellung der Schweiz als Ferien- und Reiseland trotz zunehmender ausländischer Konkurrenz bisher so gut wie unangefochten geblieben.

Du fait de sa situation géographique, la Suisse a été prédestinée de tous temps à être un pays de transit. Très tôt, des voyageurs en grande nombre ont traversé les cols des Alpes. En liaison avec la mode de vacances et de sports naissante, les beautés de la nature sans pareil ont contribué largement au développement du tourisme. Une infrastructure extrêmement variée de voies de communication, de possibilités d'hébergement et d'attractions touristiques existe à l'heure actuelle pour le repos, la détente, les séjours climatiques, les sports d'été et d'hiver. Beaucoup de lieux de villégiature et de centres urbains suisses jouissent d'une réputation mondiale. Cependant, ce ne sont pas seulement des hôtels de premier ordre et des restaurants à cuisine choisie qui sont aux petits soins d'une clientèle exigeante; des opportunités simples et moins chères permettent aux clients ne disposant que de moyens restreints de passer des vacances agréables. Comme, en règle générale, on obtient encore toujours une bonne contre-partie en prestations de service pour son argent, la position de la Suisse est restée pratiquement incontestée comme pays de vacances et de voyages et cela malgré une concurrence étrangère croissante.

La Svizzera è tra i Paesi più cablato del mondo. Numerose centinaia di gestori di rete private diffondono programmi radio e televisivi svizzeri e stranieri, a livello locale e regionale. Per decenni, la Radio Svizzera Internazionale RSI - il programma internazionale della SSR - era l'unica mèdia attiva all'estero. Oggi la SSR è rappresentata in molti programmi satelliti europei. La RSI diffonde nel mondo via onde corte e in Europa via satellite ASTRA. Oltre 700 stazioni ricevono i suoi programmi di musica e di documentari. In Svizzera la RSI offre via cavo programmi in più lingue per gli ospiti stranieri, così come notiziari in inglese.

Switzerland has one of the greatest cable network densities in the world. More than one hundred private cable operators distribute local and regional Swiss and foreign radio and TV programs. For decades Swiss Radio International (SRI) – the international program of SRG – was the only medium broadcast for a worldwide audience. Today, Switzerland participates in many satellite programs. SRI transmits worldwide via short wave. In Europe the program can also be received via the ASTRA satellite. Over 700 stations rebroadcast its music and documentary programs. In Switzerland, SRI offers multilingual programs via cable for foreign visitors as well as news in English.

La posizione della Svizzera come meta di vacanze e di viaggi

The position of Switzerland as a holiday and travel destination

Dal punto di vista della situazione geografica, la Svizzera è stata predestinata da sempre a essere un paese di transito. Già da tempo, un gran numero di viaggiatori hanno attraversato i colli delle Alpi. All'insegna della moda nascente delle vacanze e degli sport, le straordinarie bellezze della natura hanno contribuito largamente allo sviluppo del turismo. Un'infrastruttura estremamente varia di vie di comunicazione, di possibilità di pernottamento e d'attrazioni turistiche è a disposizione per il riposo, il relax, i soggiorni climatici, gli sport estivi e invernali. Molti luoghi di villeggiatura e centri urbani svizzeri sono di fama mondiale. Tuttavia, non soltanto gli alberghi di prima categoria e i ristoranti dalla cucina scelta sono a disposizione della clientela esigente; delle possibilità semplici e meno costose permettono anche ai clienti con mezzi finanziari limitati di trascorrere delle piacevoli vacanze. Poiché qui, di regola, si ottiene ancora sempre un buon controvalore in prestazioni di servizio per il suo denaro, la posizione della Svizzera è rimasta praticamente incontestata come meta di vacanza e di viaggi e ciò malgrado una crescente concorrenza straniera.

Because of its geographical position Switzerland has always been predestined to play the part of a transit country. In particular many travellers passed through the region over the Alpine passes from very early times. It was the unique natural beauty of the country which contributed so much to the encouragement of holiday-making and sport-tourism in Switzerland. Today there is an extremely diverse infrastructure of public transport and public roads, accommodation and tourist attractions available for relaxation and for health cures as well as for summer and winter sports activities. Many holiday resorts and conurbations in Switzerland are world famous. There are not only first class hotels and other establishments with exquisite cuisine for the demanding guest, but also simple and more reasonable facilities to enable people of more modest means to spend pleasant holidays. It is a fact that, in general, value for money is obtainable in this sector; and in spite of increased international competition Switzerland holds its position as holiday and tourist country as good as unchallenged.

MULHOUSE
BELFORT
MONTBELIARD
BESANCON
LA CHAUX-DE-FONDS
BASEL
DELEMONT
NEUCHATEL
BERN
LUZERN
ZÜRICH
WINTERTHUR
FRAUENFELD
ST. GALLEN
FRIBOURG
THUN
LAUSANNE
MONTREUX
THONON-LES-BAINS
GENEVE
VERNIER
LOCARNO
VERBANIA
GALLARATE